Life Isn't Just Passing Me By...

IT'S RUNNING ME OVER!

Michelle Kismoky

Argus Enterprises International Inc
North Carolina****New Jersey

Life Isn't Just Passing By.....
It's Running Me Over!

All Rights Reserved © 2009
by Michelle Kismoky

For information contact:

Argus Enterprises International, Inc.
P O Box 914
9001 Ridge Hill Street
Kernersville, North Carolina 27284
www.a-argusbooks.com

ISBN: 0-9841342-5-5
ISBN 978-0-9841342-5-0

Cover designed by DUBYA

Printed in the United States Of America

Table Of Contents

Introduction................................ i

Chapter One: *Looking In "Lost And Found"*
For Your Mind............. 1

Chapter Two: *Another Name For Your*
Mistakes........................ 35

Chapter Three: *The Battle Of Self-*
Appearance.................75

Chapter Four: *Looking At Life Through*
Twisted Glasses................119

Chapter Five: *Generation "F"*................. 155

Chapter Six: *T.T.F.N*.......................... 178

Introduction

Life is the great frontier in an ever-changing world that can, as my husband puts it, put you in a pine box and bury you six feet under before you have even begun to have a good time. But that's only if you let it .

Life is the very thing that can make or break you and play with your emotions to the point where you don't know which way is up or even the way out of the hole you dug yourself into. It is how you play the game that determines what life has in store for you.

At some point in our lives we have a tendency to tell ourselves fairy tales instead of telling them to our children. *"Everything will be all right, and one day things will get better. Tomorrow will be a better day."*

Someone has forgotten the expression, *"Same shit, different day."* They say that when life throws you curve balls, you are supposed to get back out there and try to swing again. The question is how many times do they expect you to play the game when you don't even like baseball? It's like someone telling you to get in a shark tank with a cut on your leg and see how many times you can jump in and out before you get bit in the ass. I don't know about you but I've been bit in the ass a lot of times in my life, and it is not a wonderful tingly sensation that I would recommend to have happen to you all the time. You know the saying, "If you fall off the horse just get back on it again." I think it is getting a little old, and I'm sure the horse is now ready to retire after all this getting- on, falling-off business.

I've learned how to take life's little ups and downs and turn them into laughter. Learned is the key word here. I think my sense of humor is a God-given gift that helps me get through the rough times in my life, no matter what happens to be in my way of succeeding. Not that I have succeeded an enormous amount but I have failed a lot. Well, maybe not failed. That's being a little too hard on myself. Let's just say I have been stressfully challenged throughout my life and still haven't conquered or mastered the universe.

Yet.

I don't think I have set the world on fire - maybe my kitchen once or twice - but not the world. Even so, I keep on going like the Energizer Bunny, but I'm sure the Duracell guy will catch him soon, too.

I may not have a degree in psychology, humanity, medicine, or anything like that, but I do, however, have experience in the world of the living human being on a daily basis. As for any aliens out there, you will have to write a book of your own about living in this world as an alien.

This book will not have those long words whose meanings we have to look up when we are trying to understand what we are reading. Having to have a dictionary on standby doesn't make me want to read on. Don't you just hate looking up the words in a book you are reading with topics such as, "How to Improve Yourself" or "What Kind of Person are You?" *We can fix all the problems in your life in the next thirty chapters.* Approximately one hundred pages long, the book enables you to get done in time to go to work, do the dishes, or maybe even squeeze a complete reading in before bedtime to start fresh in the morning...although I don't know how fresh you will be with tired fingers from flipping through the pages of the dictionary looking up words, and losing sleep because it took two hours longer to read it.

The sad part is after all our hard work reading and looking up words we still don't know who the hell we are or if our lives are going to be any easier. It's amazing what they put out now to simplify your life to the fullest extent. If you want to, you could even get that book on tape so you could listen to it in the car, on a walk, packing the kids' lunches, making love to your other half, or soaking in a hot bath. The kicker is that for some unknown reason we think if a doctor or a specialist has written it, the book really will be able to solve all of our problems.

How do they really know your problems without seeing you face to face? I feel I have just been lumped into a category that I have no qualifications to be in. They give us the impression that because they have all this knowledge and have put it in a book for us to read, they have no need to see us, we can just do it ourselves. *But,* let's not forget we can't do it without this book or tape. It's almost as if we need that doctor's expert advice, or at least that book or tape to justify to our friends or our loved ones, that this book or tape was written by so and so and they have led me to believe that this was my problem, so that's why I have made these changes. In most cases, we go overboard, and the changes are so drastic they seem absurd. We get uncomfortable and go back to the way we were and look for the next book or tape to try out.

Who's to say we really needed to change? Maybe we are just a little bored with the way life is going lately, and we are looking for some spice in our lives. But, you know, for the little changes that we try to make once in awhile, I just feel we shouldn't place all of our eggs in the book basket. Get out there and try something that you have seen on TV or saw someone doing in the parking lot at the mall(nothing illegal of course). I was merely thinking about skipping to the front door or grabbing your hubby's behind on the way in.

Hell, with all the unusual or elaborate people in this world, who cares if you have made a few changes in your life. If it makes you feel you are making a difference in your life or feel good about yourself for a little while, then there is no need to justify it to anyone...unless you are now wearing your clothes under your underwear. Then I can see where people may get the wrong impression of how you are improving yourself.

Those of us who have had hard or even unbearable childhoods sometimes have a hard time fixing the problem in our lives because we are not sure what's wrong; we just know there is a problem. So we consult a professional:

"Why do you think you feel that way? What are you thinking right now? Do you feel any better this week?"

"How the hell should I know? That's why I came to you - the professional for advice!"

Then there are others of us who have had too many damn problems in our childhoods and feel the talk show approach will be the ticket to joy and freedom in this world. Personally, I feel that it's a cop out to make people feel sorry for you and take pity on you for everything bad you have done in your life and have turned around to make it appear that it was someone else who did it to you. Take action for your mistakes in your life! Don't blame someone else for hurting you as a child or an adult. It is hard to find a way to pick up your own pieces, but with humor and a dedication to be a funny, easy-going person (along with learning to like yourself), you can achieve the same positive outlook on life that people who have had normal childhoods have about themselves.

What's a normal childhood?

I really don't think there is such a thing as "normal" in this world, although I suspect that it is whatever life you feel comfortable living in and makes you happy. This is probably what normal is. As for liking myself, some days are better than others\. It depends on two things. One is if I know who I am when I look in the mirror, and the other is how hard I am looking for perfection.

There are so many funny things – differences in opinions, and lifestyles - that a person is exposed to in his or her lifetime that I can't believe a person could really pinpoint what is a normal life and what is not.

I am thirty something, and I will leave it at that. I don't know when I can finish this book. I'm hoping that it will be by the end of my thirties. I enjoy life to its fullest and try to keep a **stiff upper lip** (another term whose derivation puzzles me. The thought of someone starching his or her top lip comes to mind, but I don't think that is how this term came about).

My childhood was horrendous, and the adult life has not been any bed of roses, but I make it as bearable as I can by having a sense of humor about any situation that can become too serious. I have been told that being too serious is what causes those wrinkles between your eyebrows and on your forehead. Who needs that? The Oil of Olay Company already makes enough money just from our getting older. Why give them a bonus?

I once read somewhere to trust your intuitions. The universe is guiding your life. I'm not exactly sure what it meant, but I think I would like to change the universe that is guiding my life to one that is a little easier on me. Maybe Scotty could beam me up, or perhaps H.G. Wells can put me back in time, way back when life was simpler. I don't think this is likely to happen, so I will just need to press on.

I have always wanted to become a comedian and tried out being one once at a bar. I didn't do too badly, but I was so nervous I never did it again. At the places I worked my humor seemed to keep everyone happy and smiling, no matter what terrible things have happened.

I wish to have you enjoy this experience for yourself with this book, and that way I don't have to take up waitressing again so that you could come see me. It is my hope that my terrible spelling, lack of proper English and misplacement of commas will make you feel right at home. I'm typing this on an old IBM electric typewriter. How about that for down-to-earth? I like small introductions or prologues, whatever you want to call it. Twenty page introductions never turned me on; I just want to get to the meat of everything. Yes, I tend to be a little impatient.

Now on to my book with the interesting title, enjoy.

(Update on the typewriter: I now have a computer, but that doesn't mean I will sound any more professional. It just means the spell-check will work a little faster.)

This book is dedicated to SALLY LLOYD, a very wonderful woman who always loved my sense of humor and encouraged me to do more with it. She always saw the best in everyone, even when you couldn't see it in yourself. She was my friend, my boss, my mentor, and like a mother to me. She was a phenomenal woman and will be greatly missed.

CHAPTER ONE

Looking In "Lost And Found" For Your Mind

Hormones, what wonderful things. Once they kick in, our lives are never the same. Our minds leave our bodies to fend for themselves so often we have to try to keep a journal just to see what we did the night before and keep us up to speed on how we feel from one hour to the next. I don't know why we even bother. Look at us: we can't keep our hands on the grocery list long enough to go shopping with it. We put all our time and efforts into remembering to make a list and adding to it all week long, only to have it disappear in one final swoop off the fridge and (supposedly) into the purse on the way to the store. Even if you manage to hang onto the list, you

1

still leave the store without at least one item that was on it.

So why are we keeping a journal when we can't figure out where we laid it down last? How do we expect to add today's addition about our awful trip to the grocery store or the old man at the gas station who seems to think my husband's truck is a little big for me and says, "Your daddy let you borrow the truck again, little girl"? These are important things that we really need to write down. We need a chance to read about what we've already forgotten from yesterday, but where in the world did we put that journal?

You know darn good and well that by the time we do find it, we will have forgotten what we were going to write in it anyway and what we wanted to know about tomorrow...oops I mean yesterday. By the time I find it, tomorrow will be the day before yesterday.

We lead such chaotic lives that we have to have water fountains in the house, meditation spaces outside or Zen gardens in our offices, just so we can vegetate or zone out for a while to get relaxed. We are always trying new things to make our lives less stressful, but what, overall, are we really doing to ourselves?

To me this is just practice or the first training session for our minds to learn how to leave our bodies for a moment while we distress. The next thing we know, our minds are leaving our bodies even when we don't want them to. We teach our brains to take mini-vacations, and the next thing we know they are taking longer vacations, and we have a problem.

Why? After all, we taught ourselves how to do this. It's like teaching your children how to dress themselves and once they have learned to do this we don't like the choices they're making on their own. This is what we wanted, right? But we never thought they would have a mind of their own as to how they would like to dress.

Nobody said our minds couldn't have a mind of their own, either. As we get older, our minds have learned to leave our bodies on a more permanent basis, and no journal in the world can make us remember what we did with the keys to the car. So with these challenges at hand, we improvise with

3

gadgets that are supposedly designed to make our lives easier. To find our keys we opt for those voice- activated or clapping-noise things to attach to our key rings that make squeals or whistles to help locate them. Unfortunately, we forgot to put a new battery in the gadget, so we still can't find the keys, and we are unsure where the batteries are that were bought for it.

We buy car chargers for our cell phones because we can't remember to plug our phones in at night, but it doesn't help because we always forget one or the other (the phone or the charger) on the way out the door.

My theory is that our memories start to go down-hill as soon as puberty starts, along with the daydreaming in class of the boy in front of you asking you out or getting out of school early and going to the beach. These constitute the early years of training the brain to leave the body. The only difference is that at puberty, it is a selective memory loss not an involuntary one.

I am convinced that this is the starting point for the most famous answer, "I don't know". This is the standard answer when you ask your child why they have done something that was so idiotic you can't believe they didn't have a clue as to why they were doing it. This cluelessness sets in at a very early age, like two or three *("What made you think you could mix and bake a cake on this shag carpet?")* and continues right on up to those wonderful teenage years, where the *"I don't know"* statement has been mastered *("What made you think the car would float when you drove it into the lake?")*.

Children are the best people you could ever have around you to keep you on your toes and to give you joy with a headache every day. My children have always made me laugh, no matter what they have done. Just the way they think makes you wonder what planet they came from.

I do believe that having these wonderful little children around has a hand in our losing our memories and driving us to the 'funny farm' at a very early age. I haven't seen it documented in any of those medical journals yet, but I'm more than convinced on this theory. It doesn't matter how old your children get, you will always hear their standard answer, and I know this because I still do it to my mother.

Only now I am old enough to stand up for myself and tell her the real reason. Still, I would rather say *"I don't know"* than get into a big discussion over what I've done.

In some cases, I really don't remember what my thinking was on it at the time. As we get older, we tend to get worse at remembering, staying focused, and just trying to say what's on our minds, especially when we don't know because our minds have stepped out for a moment.

This is becoming uncontrollable with a hint of downright insanity because we are now driving ourselves crazy with the forgetfulness and the stupid things we do. *"Where in hell are those damn keys? I'm going to be late for work!"*

Experts say it is the stress in our lives that causes this, but I think some of it has to do with the "Parents' Curse" that we are all blessed with by our parents for putting them through so much hell when we ourselves were children.

You don't have to have children yourself in order for this curse to take effect. It will just happen naturally, as soon as you move out and begin life on your own. For example, how about locking yourself out of your house, closing that door and looking at the keys sitting on the counter with your cup of coffee and your cell phone right next to them, as the door closes ever so tightly.

Look at the bright side; you remembered to bring the car charger for the phone. Your eyes see it but your brain never sets off the fireworks and the alarms to make you stop closing the door to go get those items you're leaving behind. If you're lucky, your friend or your other half has a set you can get easily. If not, then you're calling a locksmith from the neighbors' house... providing you know your neighbors. Nowadays no one really gets to know their neighbors as they used to.

Nevertheless, at this point it is not a question of how late to work you're going to be, but do we even bother to go at all after this drama we have created for ourselves first thing this morning. We innocently blame this on not having enough coffee, and by the look of things you are not going to get enough coffee at this rate either.

People say that we need to exercise the brain for it to continue to work properly. In my opinion, you can't teach old dog new tricks. You have been training your brain to leave your body for years just to get a little peace and quiet, and now you want it to roll over and stand at attention every time you say stay.

"A mind is a terrible thing to waste."

I believe someone famous had said this once or maybe it was a commercial on TV. It's amazing just how often we do that. We know we need to read more to keep our brains and memories sharp, but we figure watching *Jeopardy* will be enough stimulation, which makes no sense because we don't know most of the answers anyway. We certainly won't be writing them down and memorizing them for party conversations.

We watch the news just so we don't have to go out in the morning and walk though the wet grass to get the newspaper to read. We certainly don't want to get up a little earlier to read the newspaper, and if we read it after work or before bed, it defeats the purpose of reading it to see what is going on for the day before we head out.

We need to exercise to keep the blood flow going so our brains always have a fresh supply of blood.

Just a thought here: why do they say *"fresh blood?"* Do we really have stale blood after a while? And if so, shouldn't we behave like a car and get it changed every three thousand miles?

They say exercise is something we need to do. And what do we do with this wisdom? We sit on the couch watching the other people work out on the TV while we eat our doughnuts for breakfast or the large pizza for dinner with a Diet Coke.

What can I say? We all have issues, and I don't see mine going anywhere soon. How about you?

We take short cuts like drinking coffee in the morning to wake us up and make us more alert and get that brain working for us. And then we lock our keys in the car as soon as we get to work. As if we didn't have enough problems this morning trying to get to work on time! First, we had to look all over the house to find the keys, and now we may have to stay the night at work until someone gets those keys out. Well, at least we won't be late tomorrow.

We know we need to eat good meals to keep us going for the whole day. Mmmm, that *Snickers* was satisfying for lunch. Thanks to this 'no breakfast, candy bar for lunch move', I am now on a sugar high and suffering from attention deficit disorder.

This can cause problems at work when you have called a co-worker to give her a message that someone has left for her, and she doesn't answer the phone. So you leave a message about the message and she calls you two hours later asking you what you called for. She has not checked her messages. She just responded to the *"1 missed call"* number, pushed *"call"*, and now expects you to tell her what you called for. By this time that *Snickers* bar has really kicked in, and you don't remember what the message was that you called her for or what you said on the message you left on her phone. The only thing you can do at this point is listen to the message together in order to jog a few brain cells to work with you here.

We wonder why the brain is just not working correctly most of the time. Gee, *"I don't know."*

I'm just trying to inject some humor into all of our forgetfulness. At this very moment, for example, I am trying to find a little humor in the fact that the milk is in the cupboard, the cereal is in the refrigerator and it has been that way for at least three hours. If you will excuse me, I need to go buy another gallon of milk.

Ok, I am back.

Our lives are so stressed and hectic that it's a wonder we have what little mind we've got just to get by on a daily basis. I am constantly running in five different directions making breakfast, packing lunches, getting the kids off to school, husband to work, myself to work, and that's just my morning.

At work it is just like at home, trying to find help for clients or figure out what everyone has done with everything I need in order to enter the data for the statistics that are due today.

The evening is fun-filled with picking the kids up, making dinner, giving baths, doing laundry, reading bedtime stories, and hoping I still have enough energy for a little bed-time romance.

I think there are some subtle differences between the genders for some memory loss. I believe that men have a whole different reason for losing their minds. They tend to have a little more of a handicap when it comes to this problem. You see, God gave man a brain and a penis but only enough blood supply to run one at a time. You can't blame everything they have forgotten on this selective memory, but it's a good bet that's the cause of most of it. Sometimes there just isn't enough blood to make a connection from the ear to the brain. More often than not, this will tend to be the problem, especially when he is watching the babes run down the beach on Baywatch and you want him to fix the garbage disposal when the show is over.

I guarantee you the amount of blood supply needed for remembering to do this task was nowhere near the brain at the time.

There is nothing you can do unless you can tie the request to what they are seeing: *"Honey, when the show is over can you fix that bouncing silicone breast in the sink for me?"*

Then you might have something.

As for the ball games on TV and not hearing you, that is selective hearing, which turns into the selective memory. The blood supply at this point is right where it needs to be, so there should be no reason for not remembering what was asked. Just like a child, a husband can and will tune you out if it is something he is not interested in.

Let's face it, we are all capable of selective memory and hearing at any age. Professionals seem to think our memory has a lot of hindrances and stress is only one factor. Not using the brain to analyze, problem solve, or read and process on a daily basis could be why we do not retain our memories.

I am no doctor, but this only seems logical. Just like anything else; if you don't use it, it's not going to work when you need it most. They say once you learn to ride a bike, you never forget. I know from experience that I am a little wobbly on a bike after not riding one for a few years. Maybe that has to do with age more than it does with the memory; let's blame it on memory anyway. They say our minds will only collect dust if we don't use them. I have never seen a feather duster made for dusting the brain yet, have you?

You can't expect to get smart overnight or regain your memory overnight but I do believe you can improve it with little changes here and there to make it better over a course of time. I know I have a little better time with my memory now but it takes a lot of use and natural herbs to get my mind to stay on task.

I would suggest to everyone try reading the newspaper; it can't be all that bad. Well, the news will be, but reading won't be. Okay, so the whole thing stinks. Just read the comics. Actually, I find you know more about what happened in a news story by reading the article in the paper than you do seeing it on the news. I think they have to make the news on TV short because they know the whole world is watching the news more than reading the paper.

I feel that we are all still suffering from that attention deficit disorder from the *Snickers* we had for our breakfast and lunch. Reading tabloid magazines might not stimulate the truth but could stimulate you to read and use your brain a little more. I don't know about you but seeing a woman on the cover holding an alien baby doesn't strike me as truthful news. It does make me wonder, however, where the hell they come up with some of this stuff. It has to be someone with a very active brain and imagination. So, for something to read for a couple of good laughs while standing in the check-out line, yes, I would read it. I do not find these magazines that appealing but I hear there are a lot of people that do always read it. It's almost as bad as being hooked on a soap opera everyday at noon.

I don't like those either - too much fake drama for me. Last time I saw one, it took them six months to get the lady out of a hole. That's called extremely dragged-out drama. To read this or watch this day in and day out, these must be people with boring lives themselves and the best gossipers in the neighborhood, too, I bet.

They, my friends, are people that never get to leave home for a job or business duties because they are the domestic engineers of the world, dealing with the home front. They are at your doorstep as soon as you pull in the driveway, letting you know what everyone did today. The only bummer would be that there could be a week or two without so much as a nibble going on in the neighborhood.

It must be hard to be the domestic engineer these days because it's not like the movie, *Edward Scissors Hand,* where all the wives stay home and watch everything going on in the neighborhood right down to Mrs. So and so, who has every repairman in town coming to look at more than the appliances. There is an up-side to having a job these days for those of us who need gossip to be like a reality show in our lives. You can get more gossip, dirt or information at work because there is something going on every day.

Reading or waiting to see other people's love lives and affairs going on is just not as much fun as being at work and witnessing one first hand almost every day. Gossip right out of the office snoop's mouth is ten times better than reading about it. Being a waitress would be the next-best nosey job in the world. You see more going on there in one night than you can read in the tabloid. Also, people tend to trust a waitress that serves them every day more than they trust anyone else. Kind of like the bartender at the bar but in a restaurant with coffee.

Why I don't know, but people trusted me all the time when I worked as a server. One time there was an article in the newspaper talking about the carjacking in the area. Since we all worked the graveyard shift, we thought it would be a wise decision to start walking each other out when we got off before six a.m., just to be safe. One night we walked Jewel, a sweet little naive girl from Kentucky, to her truck and I asked her if she had anything in the truck to protect herself in the event someone would try to car-jack her. She looked behind the seat of the truck and said with her sweet little Kentucky accent, *"I have a roll of wall paper, some rope, a roll of duck tape and a brown paper bag".*

I could just read the headlines in the paper the next day: *"Attempted Car Jacking. A man tried to car-jack a young woman in a red truck, but thankfully she was fully prepared. The man was beaten within an inch of his life with a roll of wall paper, hog-tied, his mouth duck-taped because the woman got tired of his weeping and wailing to be let go, and he had a brown paper bag over his head because she was sick of looking at him.*

We all laughed about this for weeks. This little girl made me laugh on more than one occasion. Her husband used to thrive on her being gullible. He had called her one day from work and told her he needed the expiration date on her birth certificate before eleven-thirty to complete the forms he was filling out for his new job, and he needed her to call him back on it. This little girl comes rushing into my house with her birth certificate in hand crying hysterically because it is now ten forty-five and she cannot find the expiration date on her birth certificate.

I set her down and tell her, *"Honey if you have an expiration date on your birth certificate, then you should have a death certificate to go with it because there is no such thing"*.

Her tears dry up and she stands up, reaches for my phone to call him back and says, **"I'll kill him"**.

We laughed about this for a while and she said he would never pull that on her again. Needless to say, a few months later she was looking for the renewal date of her father's death certificate, and again I had to let her know you are unable to raise the dead.

At work I was always good at helping others with their problems, but never any good at solving my own. No matter how much experience I had, it wasn't enough to fix my own but it was great for helping others. Ever give someone advise that you yourself would love to live by but don't, and it works out great for them? You are, however, still having a hard time getting yourself to try it.

I took the turn at the fork in the road. Let's get back to the issue at hand. Back to the gossiping thing. Being nosey is one of the hardest jobs in the world, I think. You see, if you tell too many people the business of others or give bad advice, everyone will know it and begin gossiping about you. Now you are the topic of the rest of your neighbors and co-workers. Very tricky business, if you ask me. All in one simple remark the tables could turn for the worst. But you have to look at the fact they are using their brain to figure all this out. The stimulation of gossip alone will get the blood flowing really well.

The best story from when I was waitressing concerned a young man drunker than anything stumbling into the restaurant at four in the morning. He went directly to the bathroom and within a few minutes, he came out naked and lay right down in one of the booths. We had a few of the sheriff department's boys there in the back eating their dinner. I walked around back and said, *"Would you boys like to come with me? You're not going to believe this one."*

They came to the front of the restaurant and couldn't believe their eyes, either. One officer went up to him and shook him a little, *"Son, you need to get up"*.

The guy rolled over, not opening his eyes and replied, *"Not now, Mom, I just got home, and I'm tired. Give me ten more minutes"*.

We laughed, but still the officer had to get him up so he finally woke up and couldn't believe there were officers and waitresses in his bedroom. He got dressed and one of the officers took him home but this was only a reminder that you lose brain cells while intoxicated. Now this story is one that your brain will try and remember every detail, just so you can tell others about it for years to come.

Work, on the other hand, is enough of a stressful situation to make you lose some brain cells again and forget who you are sometimes. The job I have now is very demanding, and clients can be taxing to your brain. I have clients whom I would ask two and three times for their addresses, and I have them repeat it to me. Then I proceed to mail out what they wanted, only to get it back in the mail a few days later with a yellow sticker stating "Unknown Address." These are people who don't know where they live. I have come to the point that I now ask them if they have received mail at this address with their name on it in the last week. I hear a pause every time I ask this, because now they are even unsure of what they are telling me.

I have noticed that some people don't really listen either. I had a gentleman call, and right after I said clearly, *"PREVENT! of Brevard. This is Michelle. How can I help you?",* this man says, *"Hello is this Hub Cap World?"*

I couldn't resist. *"Sir, we are all out of hub caps here but we have a hell of a special going on for our programs today."*

I have been in this man's shoes, though, so I can't really say much. The stimulus for this job is draining. It's like a roller coaster. You're up one minute and down the next. Blood flow to the brain sometimes feels almost non-existent. These moments I like to call the 'brain freeze', when someone calls in and you forget your own name. *"PREVENT! of Brevard thesis..............how can I help you?"*

The people on the other end start talking, and I am not paying attention because I am still trying to figure out what my name is. Then there are other times when repetition just sticks with you no matter where you are. This creates a whole new habit for me and that is always answering the phone. *"PREVENT! of Brevard. This is Michelle. How I can help you?"* This of course is on a good day when I do remember my name but I can't remember where I'm at now. So I answer the phone like this no matter where I happen to be, at home, even on my cell phone.

I had my mother so mad one time I thought she was going to blow a fuse. See she, having the memory problem we have been discussing already, doesn't find this humorous when she calls me at home and I answer the phone as if I were at work. Now she is not sure what number she dialed. This she finds very frustrating for some reason, although I'm not sure why. Is it that she feels she has lost her mind again for the tenth time today? Or maybe it makes her feel old, and she doesn't want to be reminded of this fact. Being one of her three lovely children, I, of course, find this very amusing because I have now got her goat, but I am fifty miles away, and she can't do a thing about it. Sometimes it is good to be an adult child with power and your wits about you for the first time that day.

My mother seems to find a lot of humor in situations but there are times she can be negative about a lot of things and too serious. Don't get me wrong.

There are times she is a giant child. For example, when I followed her from the beach over the bridge to home and just as we got to the top of the bridge to go down the other side I see her hands leave the steering wheel and go up in the air. This is the only thing I see, due to her being not even five feet tall, so I can only see hands on the steering wheel and no head.

Because I know my mother so well I can hear her in my head saying, "Wheeeeee," so when we get to the stop light at the end of the bridge I pull up beside her and tell her, *"That is not a roller coaster ride. Keep your hands on the wheel."*

"How did you know that is what I was doing?"

"I could hear you in my head as I watched your arms go up in the air," I told her, *"Wheee!"*

She just grinned like a little child and took off for home as the light turned green.

At my mother's last doctor's appointment I had managed to make her laugh with my wit during a stressful time for her. For the first time, I think she understood what I meant about how you can find humor in anything if you just look for it. We had gone to her doctor to see why her heart had this little flutter in it from time to time. She was so nervous and agitated that everything she said was negative and nasty.

Finally the doctor came back with the results of her tests and started talking in terms that my mother didn't understand and frankly I couldn't make it out either. I asked him to explain it to us in terms we could understand and he said, *"Basically, she has what is called a short circuit."*

"We have known that for years," I said. *"I thought you were going to check her heart not her brain."*

There was silence in the room for a short time, but then my mother started to laugh hysterically, and that broke her worry of what we were there for. The doctor was undoubtedly a very smart man, but still it took a while to come around to what I had said. When it registered, he was laughing, too. (That is something I've never understood about very smart people: They seem to take longer to get the punch line. I wonder how long it takes them to laugh at comedy clubs.)

25

It seems we are always looking for our minds, short circuits or not. Maybe there should be a box with the words *Lost and Found Box* for your mind. I have found that I spend a lot of time checking myself out everyday just to see if I have changed my outfit, and it is really and truly the next day. They all seem to run together as you get older and busier. I figure if I have changed my clothes, then we must be on the next day.

My husband's mother has a problem, I think, with the visual connecting to the brain. She has been to our house several times in two year and she still passes the house every time she comes to visit. The sad part is that the house is located on a main road on a corner lot, and we have Christmas lights up all year so no one could miss this house. Doesn't matter if it's day or night, she will pass the house.

We are in the car coming back from dinner, and it is kind of foggy. Let me just say this about the fog first. Earlier in the evening before we had left for dinner my husband had a foregoing in the fireplace and the house was completely filled of smoke because the flue was not open. So his mother is telling him to put it out, all the while she is opening all the windows, front door, back door, anything and everything to let the smoke out. After about an hour of airing out the house we closed everything up and left for dinner. On our way out of the restaurant after eating dinner his mother says, *"Oh, it has gotten so foggy while we were having dinner I wonder what happened."*

My husband then tells her it is all her fault, and now everyone in Melbourne Florida has to suffer because she had to go and open all the windows and doors for the smoke to get out of our house. We were laughing about this all the way home because his mothers answer was, *"Really, do you think that is what all this is from?"*

During all this laughter, she is driving to our house. (Yes, yes we know. One of us should have been driving, but she insisted on driving, so what are you going to do?) Anyway, we are trying to let her know where it is that she needs to turn – *"Turn here, turn there, turn here."* There is no hope. She passes the house. She then proceeds to make a U turn in the middle of this main road, just to drive one block back and almost passes the house again. My husband is so flustered he is now getting a little sarcastic, *"What is it that you need to find our house, Mother? You have only been to this house fifty times in the last two years. Maybe I need to rent one of those spot lights like the car lots use when they are have a sale that shines up in the sky and moves around to get you to pull in the drive way. Oh, wait! Maybe I can even get it to say something like, I'M HERE, MOTHER! Would this be better for you? Could you find the house then?"*

We were all three laughing so hard that again she almost passed the driveway to the house.

It's like you brain leaves your body just as soon as the thought is put in your head, so you look very silly in front of others. Look, no matter how many times we tried to tell his mother where to turn, her brain just wasn't going to cooperate. It's just like when you're looking for something, and you never find it, but you find all the other stuff that you were looking for during the last couple of weeks.

Have you ever gotten up to get something but as soon as you leave your chair and walk two paces you have forgotten what it is you were going for? I think your brain is so comfortable in the chair it decides to stay there instead of helping you follow through with the thought it just put in your head. It's sitting in the chair laughing at you, *Ha, Ha, Ha, look at her go nowhere.*

It's not that we are stupid; it's that we have this prankster for a brain, and this makes us feel mentally challenged sometimes. Life throwing us curve balls doesn't help either, especially on the days that God decides he is bored, and he needs a little harmless humor for his day. And I end up being the guinea pig that day, waking up with the clock radio one morning playing *Shania Twain's* **"That don't impress me much"** and then waking up the next morning with the same song. This leaves me lying in the bed wondering if the day before was a dream or if I am now in the movie *"Groundhog Day"* and the nightmare from the day before is just going to continue to play over and over again. My husband says to me, *"Please tell me it is not yesterday again."*

That is life's little chuckle for the brain, and the brain loves the fact that all your synapses and neurons are going off all at the same time in fear you will have to relive an awful day all over again. Your brain is on a lightning ride with your adrenals, almost as if it were on the Space Mountain ride at Disney World, where you're in the dark being flung from side to side and dropped straight down. There are those occasions where the brain has just packs its bags and leaves, taking what knowledge you had, just because it was dissatisfied with the way you were using it.

Example: We had a man come in to my work for an alcohol screen for his probation. He blows into the test that we have, and the crystals start changing colors just a little. My co-worker, who is administering the test and filling out his paperwork, looks at the test result and nonchalantly asks him, *"Have you been drinking today?"*

"Yep," he replies, *"I had a beer at lunch."*

Duh.

Who is on probation and comes to be tested for alcohol and has a drink first? To all of us at work this was sounding like something from a *Jeff Fox-*

worthy **"You Might Be A Redneck"** joke or a *"Here's Your Sign"* from *Bill Engvall.*

The funny part is that even though we are mentally challenged most of the time, we will go to great lengths to challenge our brains some more with stress. Yes, this is where stress has something to do with our memories. Somehow we feel compelled at some point in our lives to go back to school to better ourselves. This, for some unknown reason, is something we couldn't do when we were done with high school. After all, we were eighteen and considered adults and knew everything there was to know about life.

Ever wonder what happened to those years when we knew it all? You know, between fifteen and eighteen? We felt empowered and that we deserved to live our lives the way we wanted to. Who in their right mind would need more school after spending half their life there already? We needed to go to work because we wanted money to do what we wanted to do and buy what we wanted to buy …while being paid minimum wage. We had all these grand ideas of great cars that go fast and have an awesome stereo system. A place of our own with no rules, no parents nor any idea as to how much all this is going to cost us, but we were going to have it and have it all. So, after a great struggle with our budgets, we decided to get married because two incomes sound much better than the one we were making, and of course, we were in LOVE.

After having two or three kids (including the husband), living in a cracker box, and driving two cars that together never run on the same day, working a forty-hour-a-week job, coming home to cook, clean and get ready to do it all over again tomorrow, we are now wondering if we really knew what we were doing back then. We are now twenty-something. In a few more years we start to realize the reality of this wonderful life we're living: We have two minimum-wage incomes, and we're in debt up to our ears living the American dream for more than what we make.

With all this fine knowledge that we have on what our "Real Life" status is, we decide we will go back to school to get some new knowledge in our brain, somewhere in our thirties, because we feel we have lost so much of the old stuff we have too much room in our head.

Some people even think they hear marbles rolling around up there. We also have to admit we need more money than what we thought we needed after we got out of high school.

Now let's think this out rationally. We are adults now, so we have the rational thinking gizmo in our brain. We will get up at six a.m. with the dream of an early work-out to lose weight, but instead opt to cook breakfast for everyone and pack lunches, send everyone to school or work on time, only to arrive late for our job because we have forgotten to put underwear on and can't find those damn keys again. Then we will decide to add going to school two nights awake (right after work) then the rest of the time we will come home and cook dinner, do the dishes, wash the kids, this also includes the husband or boyfriend again, get them ready for bed, make sure they are all asleep, start our homework, get at least four hours sleep before we get up the next morning and start the day all over again.

I only have one question for you: ***"HAVE YOU LOST YOUR MIND?"***

CHAPTER TWO

Experience: Another Name For Your Mistakes

We all have made those and plenty of them. If you're claiming that you haven't, you're in denial. I have made some whoppers in my lifetime, and I still look back wondering, *"WHAT THE HELL WERE YOU THINKING!"*

Now older and, supposedly wiser, I try not to do anything too stupid or outlandish to the point where someone else would ask me that question. If I do happen to make such an experience than I try to make sure there is no one around to see it. Unlike the gentleman I saw in court the other day that was wearing the same shirt he was arrested in two years ago but obviously didn't realize this. After watching the videotape of his crime and the arrest, he proceeded to defend himself without thinking about how his statement was going to look to everyone else in the room. *"That's not me. You guys got the wrong man."*

This man had a football jersey on with the number thirteen on it and his name on the back, "**Dante**", the very same shirt he was wearing in the video. I had to excuse myself from the courtroom just to have a good laugh. I also had to wonder if he was ever going to put the two together himself without someone having to tell him. I waited for a while but didn't see a glimmer of hope until his mother leaned over his shoulder and whispered. Then I saw him start to sweat and quickly pulling his public defender to his side.

This reminds me of the times you can still hear your mother or father in your head, sometimes when you're doing something so asinine and you know it, but they are nowhere in the room, just in your head. Unfortunately, you feel compelled to defend yourself to thin air: one, because there is really no one there, and two, because you're older now, and you are the one making the choices on what the hell your doing, and you'll stand firm on that (until you hear the sound of your mother's voice yet one more time, *"WHAT ARE YOU DOING? YOUSHOULD KNOW BETTER THAN THAT! HAVEYOU LOST YOUR MIND!?"* And you have the urge just to say, *"Yes, could you help me find it?"*)

I have gone so far as to look behind myself when I have heard my mother's voice, really thinking she could possibly be in the room. You see, all my life before and after having my children I had always said I would never do things with my children that my mother had done to raise me and my sisters. Then the dreaded day came where my oldest at the tender age of eight did something that triggered my mother's saying to flow so naturally right out of my mouth, *"Do you have a brain?"*

As soon as I said it, I froze, looked at my children and then proceeded to turn around ever so slowly and look behind me. Meanwhile, my children were looking at me, trying to figure out just what in the world I was doing. So with much curiosity my middle daughter, age six, asks, *"Mommy what are you looking for?"*

"I am looking for your grandmother," I explained, *"because I know I did not just say that."*

My youngest, age four, quickly came back with, *"Yes, you did, Mommy, we all just saw you say it, and Grandma was here yesterday not today. Don't you remember?"*

Children are wonderful creatures that are so innocent and bright-eyed that they never miss a beat on what goes on around them. You think your mother was good about catching you when you did something wrong? Honey, you haven't seen anything yet. These little wonders of the world will never miss a moment to catch you doing something silly, and they have the gift to make you laugh at how they look at what they have just witnessed. Sometimes I think we have a lot to learn from them, no matter how young they are or how old we are.

A lot of times I think doing silly things that are out of character for an adult makes me feel young and carefree - like my mother going over a bridge and putting her arms up saying, *"Wheeee!"* as though she were on a rollercoaster. I love running around barefoot in the rain puddles when it's lightning. My husband feels that this is redneck entertainment, and I am a redneck girl teaching my children this art.

Stereotypes. What are you going to do?

I personally don't believe in them, but they are used in this book, just for some unknown reason. Maybe it's because it is so common in this world to stereotype, and there is some humor to be had in it; that is why I used it.

Rambling again, let's get back on track.

I think we women just can't help but go off the deep end and lose our minds once in a while because of the entire "everyday life" things that are thrown at us and drain us. We are constantly thinking and analyzing what was said to us or how something was done, and that behavior puts us at the edge, and when we go over the edge, it is always considered that we have lost our minds, especially by those of the male gender.

A good example of going over the edge, or being pushed over the edge would be when we women get mad at our other half and decide to go do something extremely drastic to get back at him - like buying a new dress instead of paying the electric bill - but we can't just stop there, you know. Let's not forget once you have that dress you're going to need that sexy matching underwear set to go with it - and the shoes, too. So there are a couple more things you're not going to pay because you're so mad at him, and he deserves it. This is the part that really doesn't make sense, and I, being a woman who has experienced this, will be the first to tell you it doesn't make sense. Just examine the breakdown of it. He, after making you so angry, deserves you looking so sexy in that new little red dress and matching panty set with those irresistible high-heeled shoes?

Forget, "W*here's the beef.*"

Where's the anger? This little outfit that you have so carefully purchased is now going to be sprung on him, along with a special candlelight dinner when he gets home because you feel so good about yourself now - all sexy and very flirtatious – and this has brought you to the point where you have forgotten all about what the-hell-it-was that made you so mad at him in the first place. He, on the other hand, is going to get the most incredible evening with his lovely other half not knowing what is in store for him tomorrow when the lights are turned off and the candles will have to be used for more than just this romantic evening. The water was shut off too, so there is no way to get cleaned up for work in the morning. He won't be able to call work to say he will be late because the phone has been temporarily disconnected. The car was repossessed during all the hanky-panky, so he can't even go to work to make more money for the bills and have everything turned back on. And. in addition to all this, he has no idea you spent the money for the bills because you were mad at him.

Why?

Because you never said anything at the time he pissed you off. To think, all this was done without realizing it would just start another fight.

Wow, what lengths we women go to when we are pissed off, seeing only red at the time and not what the consequences are in the morning.

But, boy, that little red dress really looks good on me.

Men, now don't think you're not in the "oddest things we do" category. Let's talk about all those new toys and appliances you bought her for her birthday or your anniversary that she never gets to use and never wanted to use. Such as your 1970 Challenger in mint condition that no one is allowed to touch including your other half, but you will take her for a ride in it provided she takes off her shoes and there is no lint or dust on her clothing. How about the exhaust system you just bought to put in the car she is not allowed to drive, *"Honey I got a surprise for you today..."*. What about those special days like Mother's Day or her birthday when you bought those household appliances? *Ahh, that wonderful microwave.*

The last thing we need to think about on those days is how clean the house is going to be now with that new vacuum cleaner or what to cook you for dinner that evening with the new set of pans on the new stove. Let's not forget the new washer and dryer you gave her for your anniversary. Did you think she was going to get your dirty laundry clean this very second and pass on the dinner out? *("Oh,*

Honey, this is wonderful! Could we order in while I start a load?")

Trust me that will never happen.

I'm not picking on you, men, I'm just making sure you don't feel left out from all the odd things we do in our lives. This story that I am going to tell you is one I know people do from first-hand experience.

My first husband did this to me. He gave out our home phone number to the person hews having an affair with. This was not a smart move, because she could call his house when he was not home and have an interesting conversation with his wife. My husband was at a night class for electricians, learning this to become a journeyman electrician, but at the moment he was only an apprentice. I got a phone call from a woman who said she was his secretary, and she needed to talk to him... at ten o'clock at night? I stayed calm and took the girl's name and phone number. ..only to find out that it was someone that I had gone to junior high school with. We talk for a while and reminisced about school and I went on to tell her I was married to him and asked how she met him. She told me they met at a bar one night, and he just gave his phone number to her but never said he had a wife and child at home. As I remembered it, the bar night was supposed to be a study night for a final at a classmate's house. I now know another lie besides, *"I'm working late"*.

He came home and I just sat there trying to hold myself back from a mixture of laughter and anger to tell him, *"Your secretary called, and she left a message for you to call her back, and by the way, we had a lot in common. She and I went to school together."*

I've never seen someone trying so hard to think of a good lie so quickly - gears turning, eyes bugged out, and a sense of nervousness running throughout his body. Needless to say, anything he was going to come up with was not going to change my mind about what was going on. He could talk until his face turned blue and he was unable to breath and I would still not let him live, nor was I going to believe what he was about to tell me. I did, however, let him know that if he had planned on cheating on me he should have gone outside the county we lived in. Little did I know he would take this to heart and cheat on me one more time outside the county we lived in.

This whole thing I thought was a stupid thing to do on both sides of the fence: the girl for calling at ten o'clock at night knowing that she had obviously just gotten hold of the man's other half, married or not. She should have just hung up as soon as she heard another woman's voice answer the phone. The man for not having a brain in his head when he went ahead and spit out the home phone number to her. As Bill Engvall and Travis Tritt's song puts it so elegantly: ***"HERE'S YOUR SIGN"***. (If you haven't heard this song, you are missing something that will make your sides hurt with laughter.

Nevertheless, my ex-husband is going on his fourth wife; he just can't seem to get it together. In other words, he has not been able to master the cheating game or found just the right girl; maybe one more like him would be the answer.

When women are cheating, they don't get caught so easily. Women, I'm sure, tend to think things out a little more before doing anything at the beginning. After that, things tend to go down-hill. Women tell people that they think are their best friends what they are doing, but the friends end up feeling sorry for the man after a while, so they tell him. Unlike men who either kiss your ass or tell you how wonderful you are when they are cheating, women start doing things at home they wouldn't normally do. They talk back, start fights for no reason; go out with our "friends" more often. We don't want to use the men's excuse of "I'm working late". After all, we are the independent women of the twenty-first century. A woman going out with her friends is more believable. You really need to get a new lie, guys.

Then there are those women and men who think they are the masters of cheating because they have never been caught by anyone for the last ump-teen years. Would you like to know why that is? Your other half is cheating, too, so you both don't have time to think about what you are doing.

SURPRISE!!!!!

Cheating is something I have never endorsed or believed in and I have only been guilty of this once: when I was with someone for several years and he just kept cheating, so of course this woman's angry side came out, and without thinking, I slept with his best friend in our home, thinking I was getting him back. But I wasn't really, because he never found out. I never told him, and certainly his friend was not going to tell him either.

I guess if he reads this book he will now know. Nothing like confessing your sins in a book for the whole world to read and for him to find out that whole world knows now. I've made a lot of mistakes in my life, and I am not proud of them, but some were fun at the time.

As teens I think we do stupid stuff to piss off our parents and see how much we can get away with. Most of the time, it's not much. You would have never have thought that what you are doing is something your parents would have done as a teen, too. This is why you get caught, often and always wondering, *how did they know?* Now, as an adult with children pulling the same stunts, I know how my parents knew. This rational thinking, however, never crosses your mind as a teenager because you look at your parents as old has-beens who have never kicked up some dirt in their lifetime. In addition, being rational and exhibiting common sense is not in your vocabulary at this time, and the reason for this was given to me at the adolescent brain training I recently attended. The frontal lobe of the brain is not complete yet. This means nothing to you. I know, because it meant nothing to me until he put it car terms. Ahh! Give me engines, brakes, transmissions and tires as terms of explaining, and I will get what you're telling me every time. In simple car terms, you have no brakes until you are about twenty-five, give or take for the gender.

For those over the age of twenty-five still having a problem with those brakes, maybe they are on back order.

That's why as a teen your parents always asked you when you've done something stupid, *"What were you thinking? Do you not have the common sense to know that you are not supposed to do that?"*

The answer would be *"No. I'm lacking the brakes I need for that, and I just haven't had time to find brake pads that fit."*

Then just watch your head roll down the hall to your room like a bowling ball because, buddy, now you have become a smart-ass, and that is still going to get your butt in trouble. Now your butt is following your head down the hall. Pretty soon your entire body has made it to the bedroom, and now you're there for at least a week, provided you don't pull another stunt like that. Not pulling another stunt would be impossible, because your peers always out weight your mother, even if she weights four hundred pounds. Granted, she could squash you like a bug at home, but no one will see that at school. What your friends say and do to you will be heard throughout your high school for the next four years. What your mother does to you can be blown off as gossip from someone who doesn't like you because no one would have seen what went on at your house. So it's time to be stupid, but be cool while you're doing it.

Oh, the ideas, rationalizations, and priorities you have when you're a teenager! It just makes you giggle a little now, doesn't it? My oldest daughter makes me laugh. The teens today have this thing of changing their hair color every other week and putting holes in their bodies everywhere. I would come home from work not knowing what the color of the week would be for my daughter's hair. Let me tell you, we have been from blonde to blue to green to red to pink to black and now back to a normal natural color, which, if I remember correctly, was dark brown. She looked really cute with the hot pink hair.

I had the greatest moment with her the other day when I made her laugh at herself. We had gone into Wal-Mart, and while shopping for shampoo, she disappeared down the hair-color isle. She kept asking me what I thought of this hair color or that one and finally I just said to her, *"Vanity, when you figure out who you are, just let me know"*.

Another woman with a teenager was there and she was laughing about the comment. I guess she knows what I am going through, too. I know you all are sitting there saying, *why in the world would you ever let her do that?*

Well, I figured that if she wasn't running away from home, doing drugs, drinking, or breaking the law anywhere, I was fine letting her discover herself by changing her hair color. The most that could happen is it would all fall out, and she would experience being bald for a little while. Thank God that didn't happen, but little did I know it would take her two years before she found herself. The worst thing I think was coming home to the eyebrow being pierced. Worse yet, she did it herself. Luckily, she stopped at just that one extra hole in her head. It could have been worse. They could have been all over her body like some of the teenagers I see today. I wonder how some of them eat with all this hardware in their mouths and when they do eat, does it taste like metal?

When I was in high school, we did different stupid things, I guess. I had a friend once when I was a teenager, who was named Bobby, and he was so drunk one night he ran his 1974 Thunderbird right up a tree - literally. The car was parallel with the tree. When the police brought him home, and he was asked by his mother what in the world was he thinking, he replied, *"I was trying to catch a squirrel."* Not a bright answer. But that's sometimes the best you can do when you are intoxicated and being brought home by the police at three a.m. at the tender age of 16.

Sometimes doing stupid things has nothing to do with common sense or the amount of brakes you have but what you have been drinking or smoking at the time. In my day, and I'm not implying that I'm old here, high school peer pressure was a definite factor on all things you tried and did as a teenager. Now, living through my daughter's teenage years, she tries to tell me that they do these things to be individuals and not because everyone else is doing it, but they all look the same to me. I never smoked anything but cigarettes in those years, but I sure did drink a lot. Remember, I come from a redneck town where there wasn't much left to do but hang out in the Winn-Dixie parking lot and drink. I can remember coming home one night after my curfew drunker than anything, trying to get the key in the door as quietly as possible. After having no luck getting the key to work for ten minutes, I took a good triple view look at the key I was using, only to find out that it was the car key. I sat right there on the porch laughing so hard that someone heard me and came to open the door. I had thought it was my sister, and while I was stumbling all the way down the hallway to get to my room, she was laughing at me. Being intoxicated, my hearing was impaired so I thought she was getting entirely too loud so I turned to her and said, *"Shhhhh, you're going to wake up Mom, and she will be mad as hell."*0

The next morning my mother wakes me up, hands me two aspirin, sunglasses and a glass of to-mato juice and says to me, *"Don't go out drinking again until you're older - either the legal drinking age, or, better yet, not at all".*

I was just sitting there thinking how bad I felt, and I didn't think I would even want to consider drinking ever again, for the rest of my life, let alone when I was of drinking age. Then the other thing that popped into my pounding head was how could she have known? I turned to my sister and asked her if she had told on me, she looked puzzled and said, *"Told on you for what?"*

"You know. When you had to let me in the house last night because I was too drunk to let myself in."

"I didn't get up last night," my sister said, *"I didn't even know when you got home."*

Then I knew it was my mother who had let me in, and she was the one who was laughing at me weaving down the hall. No wonder she started laughing harder when I told her to Shhhh! That was also the time when I found that my body didn't respond to drugs the same way other's bodies did, and this is why I suspect I never became addicted. My first experience with cocaine was not impressive, to say the least. After fifteen minutes I fell asleep, only to wake up the next morning wondering what in the hell was the big deal with that one. I later in life tried marijuana, and found myself wide awake for two days, unable to stop cleaning the house or taking apart everything at work and organizing it to the point where people didn't know how to act when they could actually find something. What was I supposed to say, *"Sorry, it was just a onetime deal. I got high the other day, and I just had too much energy?"* I don't think that would have gone over well.

Where would we be in this world without having these experiences? As teenagers we never seem to learn what we are doing is a mistake at the time because we feel we know it all. But I also see that no matter how old we are, we just can't seem to help ourselves even when the brake pads have been installed and we know they are the right ones. I think that some of us had too much dope when we were younger, so the idiot light for the brakes is stuck on *"Dude, look at that red light. Isn't that cool?"*

Mind altering substances, what a trip they can take you on. You can blow all your money, pawn all your shit and not have a care in the world until you wake up in a cardboard box with no money and no mind left. To think people have done all this in quest of "Having a good time."

I had a boyfriend once who I didn't find out until after I moved in had a crack-cocaine habit that would eventually have an effect on our lives. I had never been around any other drugs except for the cocaine once and alcohol or marijuana the rest of the time. I had no idea that there was stuff out there that could affect your mind so much that you are unable to function. He would take one hit and instantly get this look of being petrified, terrorized, with his eyes all bugged out and he'd lock himself in the room, lying in bed with the covers over his head, unable to talk and convinced someone was coming to get him. You know how a child hides under his covers, peaking over them once in a while because he thinks he's seen the boogieman? He would sweat profusely and spend most of the evening hiding his pipe and pulling it out again.

But the only other problem was he would hide his dope in yet another place, away from the pipes, so then he would spend more time looking for the dope to put in the pipe. Then he would get on the floor brushing it with his hand all through the house, making sure he didn't lose any on the tile floor. Most of the time he would pick up little pieces of white dirt or pick at the dry-wall and put it in his mouth to see if it was his dope. This would go on for hours, and I would ask him when he wasn't high what was the purpose of doing this, and he would say to me that he does the dope to relax and have a good time from having a stressful day.

From what I could see, it looked like a total nightmare, and not very germ-free when you're putting things from the floor into your mouth. I don't think there is enough Lysol in the world to constantly kill the germs this man was putting in his mouth. He had tried several times to quit but never was successful, and I was always there trying to help him quit. I thought because I worked with addicts every day at my job, I could really help him. I can even remember a time he was avoiding one of his friends so he wouldn't smoke any dope. The guy would call over and over again, leaving one message after another, until the last message, which was: *"If you're not answering the phone, I'm coming over."*

Instead of facing the guy and telling him he is just not interested in doing any more dope, he decides he needs to go to the store for something to drink and leaves me to deal with this idiot. After the man is gone for two hours, I begin fuming with anger, but I keep myself composed as he asks if the guy came by. *"No,"* I tell him, *"but while you were gone, you missed your favorite movie."*

"What movie was that?"

"The Wizard of Oz."

"I don't like that movie."

"I don't know why not. You were one of the main characters in it."

"Oh, which one?"

"The cowardly lion." I replied.

This didn't go over well. He was a little offended but I felt better because I had the opportunity to get my sarcastic anger out and let him know how I felt about him at this time. I definitely had to leave because no matter how I tried to help him, he just didn't want the help.

I found myself having the hardest time leaving him because I did love him but I couldn't let myself be in constant jeopardy of losing my job if someone found out. The lonely nights of babysitting, making sure I was there just in case he had a reaction to the dope and he would need help so he wouldn't die was getting to be too much.

It took me six months and a few hints along the way before I actually moved out but the best hint was the day before I left. We were watching the TV and this minister, David Martin, came on and was talking about Favor and how God gives favor to some and not to others. He had explained that not always was it God's fault nor is it the things around you when your life is in turmoil or you are in a stormy situation. His example was great; he said that *Jonah's Arch* was in a stormy situation and the people on the boat were throwing off all the things on the boat to save themselves, when, in fact, it wasn't the things creating the problem, but the person who created the situation who should have been put off the boat.

"So, if there is turmoil in your life," he said in conclusion, *"maybe you should take a look at who it is in your boat and throw him off."*

I started to laugh, and my boyfriend turned to me, wanting to know what was so funny.

"Well, there's you, your father, your ex-girlfriend, the dope problem and all your friends," I said, *"I'm afraid by the time I threw all of you off my boat I would sink with my boat, so I think my safest bet is to just leave everyone on the boat and take the dingy."*

I was worried and hurt when I left, but after three months and a nice fortune in my cookie *("You emerge victorious from the maze you have been traveling in"),* I came through it just fine. It's always painful when you leave a relationship, but I think it's harder when you don't know what the outcome will be with their addiction, and you would feel guilty if something horrible were to happen.

I'm not sure the use of drugs is entirely to blame for the stupidity. I feel it might have something to do with the self-esteem of the drug taker and the choices he makes. But that is only my opinion. I don't think common sense has anything to do with self-esteem, but it might move you in the common sense area if you could see yourself in a mirror sometimes when you're doing stupid things, like taking drugs. Then maybe you would look for the help that you need to become drug-free and to just do stupid things sober. Mind-altering substances are not always present when you're doing something stupid.

Example: Under the word "stupid" in the dictionary there should be a picture definition of the man I saw the other day. He was clean-cut, dressed in a suit and tie, behind the wheel of his Lexus, sitting at a stoplight, looking very dashing...until he put his finger up his nose and started picking it where everyone could see - that is, anyone parked beside him could see.

First thing I thought was, *"For cryin' out loud, get some window-tinting or wait until its dark, but don't pick your nose in broad daylight. Here I was thinking that you're so sophisticated and worthy of a smile and you put your finger up your nose!"*

What he did with what he pulled out has yet to be seen because I had turned my head at this point so I know nothing of where that booger went. *Didn't your mother tell you when you were young not to pick your nose in a public place? Granted, you don't think of your car as a public place, but it is. If everyone can see what you're doing in it, I would think that it would be considered a public place. Scratch your balls, your butt or give a good fart in your car, just do it in a way we can't see. I'm sure you won't get very many dates like this. Especially when a beautiful woman pulls up in a convertible and looks in your direction, smiling to attract your attention, only to see you with your finger up your nose. First impressions always count, you know, or so my grandmother used to tell me.*

The only other thing I could think of was what if I had happened upon where he worked and had to look him in the eye, or the nose, and talk business? What if I had to actually shake his hand with the finger that was doing the dirty deed? I don't think I would do well; I would probably take the hand sanitizer out of my purse and a box of tissues out of my car and tell him to put both of them in his. I am not saying that men are the only ones with this bad habit in the car; it just happened that it was someone of the male gender I saw doing it that day. We as women have an entirely different set of bad habits in our vehicles, if of course we are not picking our noses or picking stuff out of our teeth before someone sees us. Getting the lipstick off is okay. It only takes two seconds, and we don't usually get caught at doing this. But digging and digging with a scrunched-up face the whole time at the light is awful. Pull over, find a bathroom and a toothpick. Let's not forget our worst habit - putting on make-up in the car. Everyone can see we are not paying attention to the road with that mascara brush in our hand and our faces plastered to the rearview mirror. Don't you know that could poke your eye out? Not to mention that the stuff burns like hell if you get it in your eyes. I can't tell you how many times I've seen women putting on their make-up in the car. Since they came up with the cordless curling iron, we are now doing our hair with those butane irons and risking major damage to ourselves. Hit a bump and your forehead has an imprint of your iron on it for the rest of the day. I'm just trying to figure out why we are so intent on trying to look good right before slamming into the ass of the car ahead of us. What are we thinking? That they might take our picture at the scene of the accident? This is not a photo shoot that will be displayed in Vogue or Cover Girl.

Well, maybe. I guess it could be a photo shoot if you have to go to the station because you have inflicted bodily harm on the person you hit, or you are heavily intoxicated. In that case it would be on the news, so looking your best may seem logical. But that isn't the case this time. You know no matter what, if they do take a picture, it is only going to turn out just like the one on your driver's license; no matter how hard we try, that always turns out to be a bad picture. I don't think the time of an accident would be the best time for a photo shoot anyway, especially after the air bag has popped out and left a red mark across your face and your eyes are all red and watery from the powder. Besides, most people are not going to care what we look like once we have hit them.

Hell, most of them now a days will rearrange your face for you, so what is the point of looking good to get your ass kicked? We might as well wear the curlers in our hair, no makeup, put on a bathrobe and just get ready for work at work. There is always the hope that someone might feel sorry for us after they see our face with no make-up and our hair all a mess. They might not rearrange our face or yell at us because we have smash into them. Hell, they might feel so bad they may be willing to take our ticket for us.

Ok, maybe that is a little too much wishful thinking, but we can always dream.

Picking our nose or putting on make-up in the car is not our one and only problem when it comes to having an accident. We also have our children in the back seat fighting, our other half telling us how to drive, or our mother in the car with us who can't hear us unless we are look directly at her. Lord, if I'd known that having three children meant one would always be left out in the cold when they were fighting, I would have had another one just to make it a fair fight. This is obviously a problem that will not be solved because I have finished having children and have been tied in a knot just to make sure.

I have, however, solved the problem of my other half complaining about my driving. I just pull over and get out so he can drive. As for my mother,

I haven't got a clue, except maybe not to talk to her unless it is at a stoplight. Somehow I don't think that would work.

Ahhhh, but, honey, let me tell you about the best accident maker. This is a no-gender, kind of like a no-brainer, only this time it has to do with male or female intellect. I see cell phones causing a lot of driving problems in my travels, and you wouldn't think such a thing as driving and talking on the phone would be that big of a deal. We talk on cordless phones at home while doing the dishes, cooking dinner, and cleaning the house. How hard could it be to drive and talk? I just can't believe that you can't have a conversation with someone and not drive responsibly, but I have thought about it and here is my take. I figure people who get a leisure call, (like, *"I'll be home for dinner around five, honey. Have a good day"*) tend to drive like an old couple on a Sunday drive.

Behind the Sunday-drivers, you have the person who gets the business call that is not going their way. *("What the hell do you mean you can't find that client's file? I need that information now!")*

They start driving like a mad person, probably because they are, and they are now out to run down the Sunday driver who looks like the person who is pissing them off on the phone.

Next in line is the person who gets the gossip call. *("Oh, girl, get out of here! She did not say that, did she?")* She is all over the road, and you are just hoping there is not another business-call person behind her.

This is my philosophy on how people drive while talking on the cell phone. This could very well be a major problem. I know offhand that I cannot drive and talk on the phone with other drivers coming at me from all directions. Lord only knows what phone call I would be up against. I hope it's the Sunday-driver. I almost feel like a football player, getting in and driving my car, dodging other vehicles pulling out in front of me or cutting me off at the pass so they can beat the car beside them to the next red light. All this just for me to get home, to the goal lines, my touchdown point.

There has only been one time I didn't score the touchdown, and I was tackled at the one-yard line.

A little girl on her cell phone, letting her work know that she was running late, hit me in the ass just as I was getting ready to turn into my driveway. So much for getting that Sunday-driver who only goes two miles an hour to hit me.

What makes us all think we are doing such a great job of juggling driving and phone conversation? I know we are always trying to multi-task everywhere; at work and at home, but it is not the same thing when you are in your car. You're already multi-tasking with all the commotion going on around you. To me, it's like trying to drive a stickshift and eat at the same time during your lunch hour or at the five o'clock rush hour in stop-and-go traffic.

You don't even necessarily need to be driving for eating in the car to become a problem of its very own. If we are going to drive and eat maybe we should pick something that is not so messy. People driving near you or at a stoplight see you struggling to put that big-ass burger or burrito with everything on it in your mouth where a ton of sauce oozes out all over your face and on to your work clothes. By the time you get to work, you look like you have had a food fight in the parking lot of Taco Bell or Burger King, and you lost the fight.

We should buy something little and easy to handle at lunch, like chicken nuggets without the dipping sauce. We all know that we cannot be satisfied with just a little bit of sauce on the nugget, we have to stuff the whole thing in that little container and make it gush out everywhere. Then we have to play the quick-bite maneuver, which is where we try to get the nugget to our mouths as fast as we can before the extra sauce drips on our face or clothing.

We really should try to make life easy for ourselves. I know it gives us less to bitch about for the day but I am sure we could find a lot more to bitch about on a good PMS day or for men LON day (lack of nooky) to make up for it. Driving while trying to do all these other things is creating more stress then what I need in my life right now, so why do I add it to my daily routine? It seems that no matter how much experience we have under our belts or how much pad is left on the brakes, we still repeat our mistakes so I'm not really sure if we are learning from them or if we just get a kick out of being repetitive.

There is nothing worse than getting a kick out of yourself when there is no one around to enjoy the humor you have just found. And then they show up in the middle of your good time with yourself and start looking for others who should be laughing with you, only to find you are all alone. Doesn't that suck? They now think you have lost you marbles, bag and all. Maybe there are times we would just like to see if our experiences, due to lack of thought, could possibly get us put up in neon lights, or on giant billboards so we can be famous.

On my travels to the wonderful states above Florida I happened upon some really interesting thoughts that weren't well thought out. Billboards are great eye catchers, but for some reason while traveling, I got the distinct impression that all southern state signs and billboards should be read and approved by northern states before they are put up. In Georgia I saw on the side of the road a small white sign for a fruit stand advertising, *"fresh peaches and Vidalia onions. Free samples, twenty-*

eight cents." If you have to pay twenty-eight cents I don't think it's free unless the price of free has gone up with the inflation in this country.

In South Carolina, there was a billboard that stated, *"Charlie's tattoos done while you wait."* Maybe I missed the news flash, but are we now able to detach any part of our body and drop it off to be tattooed? *"It will be ready in two hours; you can pick up your arm then."*

Can you imagine if it were the same type of scenario as when you drop off your car, and then at the end of the day you go to pick it up, but there have been some new developments? There was an extra charge for something, but you only had the amount of money that you were told it was going to cost? So now they won't give you your car until the extra is paid. Is this how the tattoo parlor will work, too? *"I'm sorry it took a little more tattoo ink than I thought so that will be an extra fifty dollars and you can't have your arm back until it's paid".*

There are just so many things in our lives that can make our minds go on an endless journey of 'what ifs'. In the town where I live there is a section that everyone has decided to call the "redneck" end. My husband often is convinced I was born and raised there, just because I run around in my bare feet outside and have I no problem getting under my car to fix it - acrylic nails, make up and all - becoming dirty and greasy in the process. I'm just like the kids when they come home from school. I come home from work, get out of my good clothes and put on the play clothes and out I go, under the car.

Yes, I am the new poster girl for the Betty Crocker cookbook, a wrench in one hand and a potholder in the other, on which is needlepointed, **"I try to do it all."**

My daughter has a real picture of this somewhere; I was in the middle of fixing my bearings in the front of my car and cooking a roast so I had to keep running back and forth from the oven to the car with a wrench in one hand and a potholder in the other, and my daughter caught the moment on Kodak. Anyway, let's go back to the signs in redneck land. They have all these streets with names from other countries, and we all assume the city knows how to spell the words for the street. In this case, it was evident that the redneck-in-charge spelled Sorrento Road as Sorento Road, and now this mis-spelling is as big as day on a street sign for everyone in the whole world to see that it is not quite right. You look a little foolish if you live on the street and have to spell it for someone that knows how it is really supposed to be spelled, so they automatically think you don't know how to spell.

I'm convinced the whole world is like this, but it just doesn't make it on to giant billboards or street signs, most of the time. So we now know that no matter how much experience or education you have, you are still bound to make more mistakes and create more experiences for the rest of your life. This is not meant to be a bad thought, just a little reminder so you can have a good chuckle at yourself when you do something stupid the next time. Just remember, keep it humorous, and you can screw up as much as you want without feeling like an idiot. You're just a human being in this world who is entitled to make a mistake and laugh about it by yourself, or get others to laugh at it with you.

Another thought is we might need to think about ordering a new set of brake pads. Who knows, maybe ours wear out after so many thousand miles? I wonder if they have a warranty.

CHAPTER THREE

The Battle Of Self-Appearance

HAPPY NEW YEAR!!!!!

Yes, it is that time again to make the same resolution as last year and the year before and the one before that, but this time we are going to stick to it. Let's lose weight and be healthy. For some reason we have good intentions, but it just doesn't seem to pan out. My problem was trying to achieve both weight loss and being healthy at the same time. Trying to quit smoking and lose weight is not the answer, because you are feeding your face with everything under the sun to try to quit smoking. The biggest temptation when you're trying to quit smoking is walking past the people who have just had a cigarette and thus have this aroma of smoke around them, and you find it to be a new wonderful cologne with this lovely intoxicating smell. You even go as far as to complement them on it, *"MMM you smell good today."* This makes it tough. As if anyone, including yourself, has ever smelled good when you smelled like smoke mixed with whatever cologne or perfume you were wearing! It also makes you look like you have lost your mind.

Due to several attempts to quit smoking and an array of other set-backs, I am a slightly overweight as is most of our world, but I consider myself a semi-beautiful bundle of joy. Unfortunately the world puts a lot of emphasis on how big you are, and I had realized that this was a great problem in our advertising industry, but it really struck home as to how many other areas in our lives look at this as a problem too. A girlfriend of mine was trying to get insurance for her family. She was given a simple quote without any real questions about herself or her family. After getting the information, she thought it sounded reasonable so she decided to proceed with giving the rest of her information to the representative. When she got to the question of her weight, she was told that the rate she was just quoted would have to be raised due to her being overweight. To me that was just absurd; how can you charge someone extra for being in good health and about thirty pounds overweight?

Of course, my mind went on a tangent and was thinking, *what about charging the anorexic bitch more for the harm she is doing to her stomach, her esophagus and her heart just to stay thin?*

At least if my girlfriend and I get into a car accident we could bounce off the air bag and feel good enough to get out of the car and start questioning the person who hit us. I say "questioning" because we live in a world that is entirely too violent. We all know we would love to kick some ass at that moment, but we also know it is vital to our child and society that we need to be kinder to others. That little tiny thing would have to be cut out and be found somewhere inside the air bag. Before you know it, the health insurance companies will be charging by the pound as though you were a piece of produce at the super market.

I know you don't want to do it, but let's move to the subject of big asses. Ladies (and gentleman), there is no way, no matter how you look at it, when you order a big greasy hamburger or a large pizza with an extra large diet soda that this diet soda is going to help you maintain or lose any weight. There is just no way in hell you're going to stop that fat in these things from going straight to your hips, buttocks, or those lovely thighs, even if you wash it down with a sixteen-ounce diet soda. The biggest big gulp in the world of diet soda isn't going to help you, unless that's the only thing you have for that thirty or so pounds you're trying to lose. Let's face it, you look mighty damn silly, ladies (and gentleman), ordering this diet soda with anything but a salad or by itself. You don't think the person behind you isn't wondering what the hell you're doing when you're ordering this? Trust me, I have been behind a few and look what is going on in my head.

The first thing they are thinking is: *"What do they think that diet soda is going to do for them with the large pizza with everything on it?"*

I always figured if I were going to splurge with a foot-long chili-dog with cheese, onions, and waffle fries on the side, then, hell, I should go for the high calorie drink. I'll have a beer or I would just go right on ahead and get a regular soda. Screw it, I already made the mistake of showing up at the pizza restaurant knowing that I could not resist a slice or two or three and only get a salad. Instead, I have the salad with the pizza so I can convince myself I have sort of had a healthy meal. The worst part of this is that I was at a mall and in the little restaurant area where there were clearly better healthier choices, but my big butt saw the neon sign with **"Pizza"** on it and there I was, passing up the bean sprout place and the smoothie shack made with only vegetables and fruit. Maybe there should be a neon sign on my treadmill that says "Pizza" so my butt could move a little faster on it.

I have tried for years to only eat at certain times of the day, and if I missed that time period I just wouldn't eat at all. Meanwhile my body was putting itself in hibernating mode, storing and stuffing as much fat as it could anywhere it could save it because I wasn't eating right and my body thought I was starving, shriveling away. *"Hurry! She is eating something! Get it, and let's savor what we can.*

God only knows when we will get anything again."

Stuff a little in the thighs, in the butt and let's not forget the stomach. If the inside of my body could see what the outside of my body looked like, it might change its mind about storing all that fat. I hate to tell all you folks, but from my experiences these daily binge diets and wonder pills for weight loss aren't going to work without the exercise part of it. Believe me, I have tried not to exercise. That is what the * means with the small print on the bottom of the bottle with the words, *"It won't work unless you get off the couch."*

Yes, that age-old dirty word, the big "E"; without this, no diet will ever work because you are still sitting on your ass waiting for a miracle. If you don't believe me just ask Dr. Phil. He said so in the weight loss challenge show for 2005. I have sat on my ass plenty of times waiting for that wonder pill to kick in and help me lose some weight, and, honey, let me just say it ain't never happened and it ain't never going to happen! I think the only thing that has happened is my ass has gotten flatter, bigger and there is a nice indention in my couch that is formed to my ass. Ha! Ha! Ha!

Look! The computer doesn't like the word "ain't."

Why is it that as we get older, our asses lose that rounded look? Is it because we sit on them so much? It looks like someone took a rolling pin and rolled just the bottom portion of our butt out. The worst part of it all is that they actually make underwear with padding to correct this problem and make it look as if you have a round bottom. You know, this was designed for people who never had a butt to begin with, and now we are using them so we look like we never lost our rounded butt. I guess it is there just to let you know if you don't want to work out to put your butt back, you can just fake it.

It's like when we were in school and wanted bigger boobs we either bought bras with lots of padding or we stuffed them with tissue. I personally wouldn't know anything about this, since I just woke up one morning and went from an A to a C and by the end of my senior year of high school I was a DD. When I get rich and famous I am going to find out what that B would have looked like.

Anyway, back to our butts. They really do say if you work out hard enough it will go back to the way it was, but for me it is hard to work out. I need the motivation. Not very many people motivate me, but Richard Simmons would be a start. There is something about that little curly-haired man, with the Disney-animated facial expressions, running around in his spandex outfits with such high energy and making you laugh while you're exercising that makes me want to get up and move. I think he has the right idea about moving to lose and having a sense of humor while you're doing it. He makes it look as if it is actually fun. Even if you started out dreading to move one of those hefty legs of yours, for just one second he made it seem effortless and before you knew it you were all done, wondering if you'd actually worked out for the whole thirty minutes.

After that I wanted to do more but it just wasn't the same doing it by myself without him on the TV motivating me. Now they have Billy Blanks with

Tae Bo. He doesn't make you laugh, but he makes you feel as if you could go out and kick some ass after his work out.

But the real truth of the work out comes out the next morning when you are so sore you can't even kick your own ass out of bed. I know the word "exercise" is not what you want to hear when you get up in the morning or come home from work, but that is what it's going to take to get that fat off. I should know. I have tried everything from pills to only eating salads all day long. I have even tried drinking my eight sixteen-ounce glasses of water - or is it six eight-ounce glasses of water, - whichever it is, every day with a capful of vinegar in it.

Everyone has something he or she has read somewhere in a fitness magazine or Woman's Day that he or she has tried or is going to try, and tells you about it in hopes that you will want to try it too. I think it is the guinea pig test that the magazines use trying out new stuff, to see if it works. They put it in their list of articles and wait for us to write them a letter telling them whether or not it worked. These magazines always have something about losing inches or pounds fast, and there is something new every month so you'll buy and try. This is a good thing if you look at it in a democratic way, because if you don't lose the inches or the weight the way you want to after you have tried it for a day or two, you can always wait till next month's issues for another shot to lose weight. I say a day or two because we as a rushed society never give anything longer than two days. Ask for a commitment of a week or a month and you'd think you have just asked people to book their calendars for the rest of the year.

How many of you have tried the cabbage soup diet? The one where you have to eat the soup every day for seven days at every meal during the day, Breakfast, lunch, dinner, and snacks. I have never been so bored with eating food in my life. Until you have eaten the same thing day in and day out for seven days straight, you can't imagine how your body reacts to this. Your mind tells you, *"NO! I won't eat it anymore"* and, like a two-year-old, your mouth puckers up as if it's going to make damn sure that stuff on that spoon is not going to get in, no matter what. At this point you can't foresee eating anything at all; not even cheating on this diet is appealing. Until you have not eaten anything but that soup for the last four days, and temptation is everywhere at this point. While driving home you spot that wonderful glow of a Taco Bell sign. That's it. You have lost all self-control. Hot sauce, refried beans, and sour cream win out every time. Don't forget to pick up a diet soda, because your body is going to be storing all that fat from the burrito you are eating due to your not eating anything but cabbage soup the last two days.

I'm being sarcastic here; just get a regular soda. You have already blown it by getting in the drive-thru with no way of getting out but by going forward. I have spent so much money on diet stuff. If I had a dollar for every pill, shake, meal, or snack bar I have bought, I could as rich as the people selling me the snake oil (this is an old term meaning "something created that was never intended to work").

In the weight game, I had to stop and take a look at where and how I got those extra pounds in my life. There was having the three kids and then hitting thirty. Let's see what else was there? Oh yes, there were the men. If I had known then what I know now, I would have gotten rid the men in my life a lot sooner and kept the kids. I have had more fun with my children then I have with any one I have ever been with.

When you have someone who is supportive, this probably would not be a factor. The same would be true if you had someone who would love to walk with you or exercise with you or even just loved you for the way you are and amused you every time you went on a diet.

I personally would like to have met the one who would amuse me, because I really don't like to work out, and sticking to a diet is very hard at times. I feel I get plenty of exercise at work as I run up and down a hall and climb stairs in high heels all day long. Then I come home, run around my house after work just to clean up and start dinner, still in those heels. After dinner I clean up again and get everything ready to do it again tomorrow. By the time I'm done, it is ten o'clock at night, and by the time my body catches up with my brain, it's eleven-thirty, close to midnight, when I fall asleep. Do you really think I would like to do an extra workout with my tapes, that I paid a bundle for, or walk around our neighborhood hoping not to get mugged?

Na. Working out at this time of night would only lead to more energy and staying up way past midnight to wind down. I have found when you have someone in your life who would rather keep your time tied up with housework, waiting on him or her hand and foot along with other things, you just don't find the time for you anymore. Yes, granted some of that is my fault for letting him get away with that but I have always thought the old-fashion way of doing things was the way to keep a relationship good.

Wrong!

It only means that you can be taken advantage of easily, without appreciation, and the support you need is not there. In my case the supportive person finally showed up, and now I'm just trying to get used to the idea that he loves me just for me and not for what I look like. Before I found him I had to reevaluate myself and push myself without home support and just the support of friends and co-workers. It seemed that before I found this husband, every person I had ever been with had consumed my time to the point I had no life of my own. I had to learn to take hold of my own life and be in control of me. Let this be a warning to all: if you are unable to keep up your appearance, shave your legs, put a little make-up on once in a while and know who you are as a person, then it is time to fix it, move on, or be unhappy and unable to know who you are every day.

I think the last straw for me was looking in the mirror and saying, *"Who are you? What did you do with that young vibrant woman who loved to live life to its fullest?"*

In my situations I stopped doing anything fun and just pushed though life and never went out to places that were fun. I worked, cleaned house, and went to bed. I even started to have a hard time having fun with my kids and that to me was a big problem, since they were worth the world to me. I would go to work the next day and by 9:00am I would tell my friends, *"It has been a long day. It's been going on since yesterday, and the only thing difference is, I have changed my clothes."*

That's when I knew I had to take another look at myself. I found, through self-discovery, that I tend to lose weight and both look and feel better without anyone in my life, and I never could understand why until I had a chance to sit down and look at it. For one thing, I always thought I was miserable being alone, but in reality, living on my own was actually better. I didn't eat heavy meals. I had time to pack my own light lunch. I also did what I wanted - walked on the beach, went thrift shopping, worked out with videotapes in the morning or at night. If I wanted to go to Wal-Mart in the middle of the night, I could. My biggest downfall was feeling so lonely I would throw myself fully into a relationship and then let him suck me dry before I realized what was happening...all this to just end up feeling lonely again, even when I was with him, because now I missed me and that was why I had left the relationship before this one.

What a world! Find yourself, lose yourself, find yourself again, lose yourself again, and now have no clue what box you have packed yourself into, but you know it is in the storage unit somewhere.

Men, however, are not the only reasons I have gained weight. It just feels good to blame some of them once in and a while, especially the ones that only wanted me if I looked good enough. Just as soon as I didn't look good enough anymore, they kept me around because I did it all, including going to work and paying the bills while they were out cheating or doing their own thing.

I can remember a time that I had a boyfriend for seven years, and every time I turned around, I had to move because he had found some young little thing who was going to be better than what he had in me. He did this to me three times, and I moved three times.

Yes, yes I know. Once would have been sufficient, but I was so lonely and in love (this is sarcasm)... lonely yes, but in love? I think it was more insanity then anything. Someone find me a ticket to Chattahoochee. It's probably not funny that I had done this three times but there is only one time that sticks out in my head and it was when he had said to me, *"I'm sorry but I have had a better offer."*

I couldn't believe my ears. It sounded as if the relationship he was embarking on was a great business deal. The only thing I could come up with was, *"I hope it pays well and has better benefits."*

After a few weeks, I had gained about five pounds and hadn't left the house, except for work. I have grown a lot since this relationship, and I know this because he called me right before I got married to tell me he was thinking of moving to Arizona and wanted to know if I wanted to go with him. I know you are just dying to know my answer. My reply was, *"I don't think that this would be a good idea. At least here when you decide to change your underwear, I have some place to move to because I have my family and friends for support. Are you going to pay the expense for me to go home every time? I don't think so."*

My answer was **NO!**

Are ya proud of me? I am. You know, I have always been moderately overweight since the eleventh grade. Before that I weighed a total of ninety-eight pounds, soaking wet. I wasn't really happy with that look either; looking like a popsicle stick with two watermelons on top just isn't comfortable for me. But you know I never really hit rock bottom with my weight until I started staying at home in my second marriage to be a housewife raising the kids when my youngest daughter was born, and I became so obsessed with my weight gain that I lost sight of reality and became very depressed. Then the day finally came when, during all the everyday chaos, I got a really good laugh out of myself.

I'm telling you, being able to laugh about your weight is a depression reliever all by itself. I woke up one morning and decided I would weigh myself, just to see how bad the damage really was before I started my one millionth diet. I stepped on the scale and low and behold I ONLY weighed 190 pounds. I thought to myself that I hadn't weighed that since high school and the scale had to be wrong. I just knew I weighed more than that. It took me the whole morning and part of the children's naptime to realize that it was 190 lbs, not 90 lbs! At this point I felt I needed to look for a really good diet, and maybe a good psychiatrist while I was at it. All the laughter and the tears that were coming out of all this were not normal. I'm sure it was a nervous breakdown of some sort. No matter, it sure was funny and it knocked me right out of my depressive slump.

When I was with someone I had plenty of time at night to work out to a videotape or walk around the neighborhood, because I was by myself most of the time. But I was too worried about what he was doing when he said he was "working late," or I was just too tired after rushing around cleaning up everything to make it look perfect and cooking a home cooked meal that he could eat after "working late", even at 2am. What a life, huh? To think men gave up a prize like me just because I was overweight.

A friend of mine used to call me the 18th century woman trapped in the 21st century because I would cook, clean, wait on the one I was with hand and foot, and even take out the garbage. The men in my life had nothing to do but go to work, cheat and come home. The things we do for a man are astounding. At some point in a relationship I didn't even know who I was. But I was always working on it one day at a time.

I'm sure you're probably wondering if I have found myself yet. I think I have found half of me and if I don't lose some weight soon I'm going to find the other half faster than I want to.

Speaking of the diet craze, I feel we have to start being a little more realistic about how we are doing it. Let's face it, you have to walk or move in order to lose weight, and you have to be able to motivate yourself to work on it. Unfortunately, Richard Simmons doesn't live next door, so that motivation is out of the question. If you're moving and not losing, it might be all those chocolate bars and dinners you're eating after you work out.

In my case, I hadn't actually gone to work out. I just was thinking about going to work out. It's stressful. You know, there has to be some comfort somewhere. So I'm a chocolate freak and can't live without a bar a day. I know you can't just cut yourself off. It's like trying to quit smoking cold turkey. You wander around walking past people that are

smoking and you want it. It's the same for chocolate. Just walk past something chocolaty in the su-
permarket or at the bakery and you want one.

Chocolate is something you just have to ration-
alize differently. You have to make a better time to
eat and enjoy it. Before you go on your walk or exercise to your tape, you can just reward yourself before you get started. This way you can still have
what you want to eat, only in moderation, of course.
See, there are ways of cheating and getting away
with eating what you want, but you just have to
make it look like you know what you're doing.

Easy rule to remember: Do not eat after six
p.m. This will make your life much simpler, your
butt a little smaller and your tummy won't feel as
bloated at bedtime. Everything in moderation. Remember, if you eat twelve candy bars before your
walk, you can't possibly add enough to your walk
that will take that all off. If you do try to add more
to your walk for eating those twelve *Snickers* bars,
plan on not being home for the rest of the night. Just
keep walking!

Those of you, who have joined a gym to lose these unwanted pounds, try using the machines. I've seen the men and women who come and sit on the stationary bikes or the benches and just watch what everyone else is doing. This is not a workout. You might as well have sat at home, turned on the workout channel and watched, while sitting in the comfort of your own home eating your *Bon Bons* on your couch.

The stationary bike is a tough one I know, but even though that word stationary is in there, and it doesn't seem to move, it has pedals to push and that is the one part of the bike that does move for you to exercise.

Speaking of bikes - the ones that aren't at the gym - why in the world would they make such uncomfortable seats? Once you have spent $200.00 on the bike you have to spend another $30.00 or more on a new seat that doesn't kill your pelvic bone or your ass just to get in a little exercise. I mean, no matter how big or small you are, you can't even see the seat because it is conformed to fit inside the pelvic area and buttocks. This, to me, is like wearing an uncomfortable thong. I'm not sure if there is such thing as a comfortable one but you get the gist of what I am trying to say here. I'm not sure who designed these seats but I think it is time to rethink this design.

Another no, no for the public gym is to work out in spandex. Honey, if you're there because you don't like the way you look, for God's sake do not squish it into the spandex until you do like what you see. I personally don't like seeing my cellulite dimples on display. Nor do I like for everyone else to see them either. This goes for shorts as well as Spandex. I would rather wear the big baggie sweat pants than have others see a cellulite dimple winking at them as I work out. I wouldn't wear a bikini on the beach, either, knowing I have a road map on my stomach from having had three children. I'd fear someone coming up to me as if I were a tourist attraction map. The whole time they were staring at me I would be thinking they thought I looked good in the suit, only to find out they were just using my belly button for the "you are here" portion of the map and my stretch marks as the roads to travel to the concession stand or the pier. This wouldn't exactly make me feel sexy in that bikini. My advice is to wait until you're confident enough to wear that bikini with all the other *Bay Watch* swimmers on the beach.

I really think they need to split the beach in sections by age, so we would all feel more comfortable. We could have the senior section for those who are wrinkled and wish to get tan to look more like leather than a wrinkled white shirt that needs to be ironed. Then we could have the middle-aged section, where those of us who have road maps from having children could be comfortable without having to watch our husbands drooling over the college students with the perfect bodies. Then, of course, you would have the section for the high school and college students, where they don't have to be harassed by our husbands, and they can have a good time with guys their own age. The last section should be given to those that have had plastic surgery to look younger and where everything is back to where it was before they had the children and the cheating, middle-age-crisis husband. This section is where everyone touches each other in a tender manner, and it's not because of the brittle bones underneath the façade but rather what they have used to make you look younger.

Just think, if someone grabbed your face the rough way they used to in the old movies to plant a kiss, your chin implant or cheeks could be readjusted in a not so flattering way. Those breast implants could be another danger. Someone could squeeze too tightly and deflate that sucker. I think this section should be called *"trying to capture a time long gone that will eventually catch up with you again."* Here you could expect to walk around like a china doll, never to be touched, only seen.

As for those spandex suckers you choose to wear at the gym, you need to be real sure they are not going to split from the seam and come off, blackening some one's eye or putting them in a coma. I would strongly suggest if you're not sure, don't wear them. Sometimes that spandex gets to be scary when you're in the aerobics room with one stretched to the limit right in front of you bent over just stretching for the warm up. I didn't come to get a black eye or to be knocked out by your spandex before I ever get to work out. Can you imagine actually putting someone in the hospital because your spandex went flying off like a slingshot across the room? What would you say? *"Oops! My bad"*.

As tight as some of these things are, it's incredible how we seem to have squeezed ourselves in to begin with. They must have a clothing horn somewhere like the shoehorn. Unable to breathe after squeezing into this wardrobe, we have no choice but to hold onto what oxygen we have left. Bend over, and you'll cut off the oxygen supply. Don't forget to walk like *Morticisha* from the **Addams Family**, or you might split a seam.

It's a wonder we can even work out at all. Maybe just move your arms. Too much movement could make you get out of breath and pass out. It probably was a good workout just getting into those clothes, so why even go on the machines at this point; you could finish your workout by trying to take those suckers off. How do you take in that breathe when you touch your toes? You know how they always tell you to inhale on your way down and exhale on your way back up? How can you exhale if you can't get anything into your lungs to breathe out on your way down?

Men, you are not left out in this. I have seen you in similar situations, and believe me, when your belly sticks out over the sides of your weight training belt it is not an attractive sight. Let it loose so it all blends together and it doesn't look like your trying for the washboard look with the tiny waist by squishing in the bottom and pushing it to the top. If you're there to meet chicks, this is not the look most women would find desirable. Love handles are great but when you add the Spandex britches and wrap that weight belt so tight that it now becomes the love spare tire from a 4x4 truck, most women tend to think it's a bit much.

Personally, I find that I am attracted to the *John Candy*-type big man who could wrap his arms around me, making me feel safe and be comfortable in the realization that I have a spare tire for my truck. For some reason, I just happened to end up with one that has a *Jim Carey* body but he still wraps around me, snuggles, and makes me feel comfortable. It's just that the spare tire has been reduced to a rim with no tire. Therefore you can feel those bony hips a little more.

I find that for some reason I am not attracted to the man who looks like someone stuck an air hose up his ass and forgot to turn it off. Have you seen these men? They can't even put their arms down, and their legs are too far apart because they can't put them together. They walk like they just got off a horse or because of the size of what's between their legs. This, however, I have been told is wishful thinking. So I guess if you're looking for *John Holmes,* it is not in this package.

Ladies, if you're shopping for a man in this crowd, you're already in competition with his vanity. Just remember that. These men who are at the gym looking really good who spend their lives at the gym know they look good and tell themselves every day in the mirror. They aren't looking for a mate for life in there; they are looking for the anorexic chic as the trophy for their arm. They are not drooling over that spandex that you have stretched far beyond the test they passed for endurance. These men will look for you when they get older, have stopped working out and wear the same size bra you do. By then you hope you will look like a million bucks and are searching forth buff guy with ripples in his stomach.

Just to go off the beaten path for a minute here, spandex, by the way, is not the only garment abused; support hose go through a beating, too, by all those women who use them to squeeze everything in to get on the dress that is two sizes too small. I don't think the manufacturer had reshaping in mind when they designed them. I know they say that on the package but I'm sure that was just a selling technique, and they didn't really mean it. Then there's the girdle that has been popular since the corset was invented. Both these items were definitely designed for reshaping with no airspace. It's amazing what we do to torture ourselves to have that certain look at any cost. Not being able to breathe or sit down would be a couple of those costs. Do you know there are women out there who wear a corset to shrink their waist size just to get that hourglass figure with a nineteen-inch waist?

They even admit to feeling the discomfort and being unable to eat anything but tiny bites of a meal. This to me is too high of a price to pay.

A woman, believe it or not, invented this ultimate discomfort in 1825. This woman was *Mary Brush* and this should tell you how long we have been constricting and harming ourselves for that certain look.

Do you know a man by the name of *Michael Soloman* invented another garment we all bitch about having to wear: the bra. Although when dressing up for a sexy evening the bra is not that bad, they don't stay on long enough for discomfort. For an everyday item they could be a little more comfortable.

You didn't know you would be getting a history lesson did you? This only goes to show you that the age-old quest to get the "right" look for the times has been going on since the beginning of time. It's no wonder we are all going off the deep end when it comes to how we look. At this rate we will never be happy with our bodies, and our children are learning from us that this is an important part of our lives. We are all dying to be thin. Literally.

My theory is that we should all look at the person inside, not the person outside. This is just a shell. It is not who we really are. It's our personality and mannerisms that make us who we are. Just remember the shell part is what eventually gets buried six feet under to be nibbled by millions of tiny insects, or burned up and put in an urn.

Now there is a way to lose some serious pounds. God doesn't care what we look like, just who we are and what we have accomplished for the betterment of ourselves and the people around us. When you go to meet your maker, He (or She) doesn't separate us by outsize, *"102 Lbs stand in line one, 198 Lbs goes to the end of the line, 298 Lbs - do we have a further line than the end?"*

Unfortunately over 90% of the population think it's all about looks, and that's a damn shame. They are missing out on some of the best people.

Like ME!

To get out of a depressive slump about my weight I say to myself *"Self, Marylyn Monroe was a size14, and men were goo- goo eyed for her so I must be just as fantastic".*

I had a boyfriend once who seemed to take longer than a woman to get ready. With that long hair and trying to dress a certain way to look great for the women. Yes, this is the same one that I moved in and out on three times. He was always on the prowl for the next best thing even with me around. He was so proud of his long hair and so hung up on his looks you just wanted to slap him. Kind of like *Cher* in **"Moonstruck."**

SLAP!

"Snap out of it".

Having no hair myself at this time in my life, I find it alarming that he has to have his hair and everything just perfect to go out. It's almost as if he has more estrogen than he wants to admit to. It's kind of scary seeing a man having women issues. There are a lot of guys out there like that, too. **"You're so vain"** should be their theme song.

Having no hair was not a problem for me. It's the idea that society has of how I am supposed to look that bothers me. You know, the "I don't feel so sexy around you" feeling.

Before I go any further I guess I should explain why I have no hair, huh?

See, I had breast cancer at this time and I had chemo treatments that robbed me of my hair, and I do mean robbed. If I'd had a choice, I wouldn't have given it up. The up-side to this was I didn't have to shave anywhere any more, even the little kitty down there was bald, if you get my drift. I found I could get out of the shower and be on my way with a wig that was already styled for me in a matter of minutes.

Those of you who have short hair for the convenience of it all; you haven't seen anything yet until you've gone bad. Shave your head one time, you'll see. I didn't even have to blow dry or pull out a curling iron. This was not a bad thing for me; scary, yes, but not bad. I took it all in stride, so don't get all sorrowful now. I have a great sense of humor about the whole thing and a positive outlook. The only down-side to the wigs was they were very hot and sometimes uncomfortable. You can't sleep in them, so therefore you will not look sexy enough in the morning to get laid or even at bedtime, for that matter.

This is where the way you look has been etched in my brain as being so very important. So I would need to get up before him in the morning to get some hair on, draw in some eye brows, and a little make-up – minus mascara, because I had no lashes - to look like a million bucks and ready for action. Up-side, my hair will look automatically better than yours waking up in the mornings. You now know what it's like to be a woman with a bald head and body. I would have loved to be able to stay bald from below my nose down just so I would not have to shave or pluck hair out of my upper lip ever again. But as far as being bald with no eyelashes or eyebrows, I think once was enough for me. Luckily, I didn't lose my breast, but it did have a scare and is slightly smaller than the other now. I used to be bothered by this quite a bit and still am sometimes, but I have since learned to have a little humor about it. I tell people to just look at them separately; the right side looks the way it did before I had children, and the left side is what it looks like after having three children. So I turn to the right and say before and turn to the left and say after.

I had spoken to my surgeon to see if there was ways to make them both look the same. He asked me how I would want them to look and I had told him I would like them to look like *Pamela Anderson's.*

He said, *"But those are double D's."*

I replied, *"So are these, but they don't look that good."*

After careful thought I decided I really didn't want more scars, so I didn't go through with it. I did take the doctor's advice. He had told me to buy a push-up bra and then they would both look perky again.

With men who are bald there is not any difference for them day in and day out. There is not a morning that goes by where they look any different in the morning than what they looked like when they went to bed. This is accepted all over the world though because for a man to be bald is not out of the norm. Now that is an up-side for you.

As for toupees, I wouldn't think you could wear them to bed either without your other half waking up to a hairy beast attacking her in her sleep.

Then there are the men with gray hair that dye it or pull it out. What is up with men and the gray hair? Stop pulling it out. Women love it, and your ego is getting the better of you. Just look at *Richard Gere, Sean Connery* or *Sam Elliot*. These men are still very sexy.

For men who still let their hair grow long in the back to take care of what little there is up front, *STOP IT!* It looks just as ridiculous as you feel putting it up that way every day. Be a man. Live with it, for cryin' out loud. If you feel you look like a broken-down old slob, take a hint from the women: Go shopping. Get a different wardrobe. Dress with the *James Bond* look or the *casual-but-I-have-class* look. For Pete's sake, buy a pair of Docker pants. Men always look good in those no matter what.

Buy dock shoes or casual dress-down shoes that are similar so you don't have to wear tennis shoes or work boots all the time, guys. Nothing worse than seeing a well-dressed man in a bar or restaurant and look down to see the sneakers he has been wearing since 1978.

Most men could probably use a good woman to go shopping with them, just to help coordinate the whole outfit, including the weekend look. Also socks with sandals do not look very fashionable, it makes you look like a tourist from the fifties, no matter what state you're in or how old you are.

Take a look at some of your well-dressed friends or the well-dressed neighbors that are getting the hot dates. You could look good only if you push yourself and feel good, too. Take a shower. Comb your hair. Look civilized, even if you're not.

For women, fashion is something some know well and some don't. For instance, take those jeans we think look sexy because they are tight. We love to look sexy, but we can't breathe or eat the dinner our date just took us out to. We wear bigger shirts to cover the overhang of our tummies sticking out. All this to look sexy and kill us all in one breath, that is if we could breathe.

Push-up bras are another thing we wear to impress men. Take it from a woman with a big chest, if you already have a big chest, do not wear this bra in a low-cut shirt and bend over. It not only pushes you up but out and, in some cases, right onto the table. This can be a little embarrassing if you're there to impress and not come undressed, especially if you don't really know the guy. Serving your breast in your customers' soup doesn't look suave, sophisticated, or even professional.

The things we do to get a good-looking guy seem very stupid in hind-sight. Women are always looking for the *James Bonds* of the world and men are looking for the *Pamela Lee Andersons* of the world. Unfortunately, we are all trying to impress the other sex with this fantasy in mind. We make up who we wish we were instead of being ourselves and are very disappointed when the person we are dating finds out we are not that person or we find out they are not the person they said they were, either.

Language seems to be our biggest barrier and I don't mean speaking a totally different language; I mean understanding what is being asked or said to you.

Men, when women ask you if you are active and out-going we are not asking how often you like to have sex or how much couch time you have with the TV. We mean, do you ever get out and walk or go to theme parks. Maybe even ride a bike once in awhile. This is the definition of active. Are you out-going? This means do you have a social life with friends and family, like parties and barbecues? Do you get along with everyone, or do you argue with everyone? Are you more of an introvert or an extra-vert?

Women, when men are asking what you like to do, they don't want to know about shopping for shoes and dresses, or having your hair and nails done. They want to know whether it bothers you if he watches football or NASCAR or, even better, do you like it, too? You should also stick to short ex-planations. If your answer doesn't pertain to foot-ball or racing, take longer than a minute to answer and you have lost them. The attention span is limited to yes or no questions, not taking over the whole conversation throughout the date.

Men, this is also true for you. Do not talk about your ex- and how much of a bitch she was or how badly she treated you. You lose the woman's attention at the *"My ex- was such a........"* We hear nothing after that and usually start scanning the room for other available men.

Women, this goes for you, too. If you start talking in the realm of something men know nothing about, they will tend to look around and see what else is going on. Talking about how you spent all day trying to find something to wear and trying to get your hair to cooperate before the evening is an absolute turn-off. *"My hair just wouldn't cooperate tonight. Does it look okay to you?"* After he says yes, do not continue going on with this conversation about your hair.

We, as a whole, are complicated people. Having intelligent conversations is a stretch in most cases, depending on whom you have picked for your date or where you are meeting these people.

Dating is just too complicated, and it is something I would not like to be out there doing again.

I read somewhere that men are like fine wine. They all start out like grapes, and it's our job to stomp on them and keep them in the dark until they mature into something you'd like to have dinner with. I thought it was cute but in all seriousness, men, if you're going to pick the twenty-year-old that wears a size two over there with all her friends giggling as if they just came from high school, don't expect to have a real conversation or even former to understand what you're talking about at dinner.

Women, if you choose the young hunk with the washboard stomach and a limited vocabulary like, *"That's cool, dude,"* there may not be a conversation there that you can understand.

It's how we choose our dates and what we are looking for in our lives at the time that determines whether or not we have a good time. If all you want is a good lay, those are probably your best choices. But beware: clueless people I don't think tend to make great sex partners. You lose the passion with every breath of *"What do you mean, go this way?"*

Or *"I don't understand what it is that you want met do."*

The best one is the big burly guy the woman picked to take home who, it turns out, only has a two-inch penis, and all her dreams of having an outrageous orgasm have been shot down. You see the big guys don't always have the big you-know-what's. Just because they build up all that muscle up top doesn't necessarily mean the rest is built the same.

The sad part is the little guy you passed up in the corner, the one you passed over to your friend, could have been your dream come true. You get a phone call from your friend in the morning telling you how great he was, and, to add insult to injury, she says, *"He could be the next John Holmes."* Now you feel worse than you did before.

I think we women need x-ray vision more than Superman does, especially if we are trying to take home a good one-night stand. We should be able to pick by size, too. After all, men can pick by the size of women's breast a lot easier than we can pick a penis.

While we are on the subject of picking by penis size, there was a night I went out with my friends to a pub. There were some young men that had staggered in from another bar, and they were kind enough to share everything about themselves. With a digital camera in hand, they had disappeared to the men's room and proceeded to take pictures of their penises. After returning to the bar from the restroom, they were so proud of themselves, they decided to pass their camera around with the masterpiece on it for all of us to see. This was the best pick up line I had seen yet. My friend and I started laughing even harder when the song **"Rocket Man"** came on from the jukebox at the precise time that the photogenic penis on the camera was passed around the bar for all to see. I'm sure they were looking for a possible young lady to take home, but the only taker was a fifty-year-old woman who is a regular at the pub.

Without having pictures to go by, I guess men could be left with bras full of stuffing or some sort of a fantastic push-up bra, just as we women could be left with a sock of considerable size. You never know until you take it home and unwrap it. Kind of like Christmas. You can't wait to unwrap that gift from Aunt Myrtle, and when you unwrap it, you are very confused about what to do with that newfangled thing that's for the kitchen. You can't even figure out why she would give you something without instructions on what it's supposed to do for you.

As for the date we just brought home, all I can say is, *"It's a HARD evening with a WET uneventful ending. Don't you think?"* After all the drama for the evening, you are left to wonder what was the point of this night while you are busy satisfying yourself to calm down after getting all worked up for nothing. At this point in my life I am happy with everything just the way it is, how my face looks. My weight is fine at 192 lbs, so long as I am healthy and my husband still feels I'm beautiful and wants to fool around with me, it's all good.

Something for all women to get a chuckle out of: Men are like parking spaces...all the good ones are taken and the rest are handicapped.

CHAPTER FOUR

Looking At Life Through Twisted Glasses

Things in life sometimes are not as they seem. If we look at life a little differently rather than through the rose-colored glasses we were given, we may get a broader view of the whole picture. Take, for example, the picture my husband had in his head this morning after finding out that for the last three years he has been drinking decaf coffee. He had innocently enough taken the empty can of coffee out of the top of my garbage can to put some nuts and bolts in it from the garage floor. When he went to put it on the shelf, he read something disturbing on the side of the coffee can.

"DECAF"

"What does this mean, 'decaf'?" he asked me, *"Does it mean there is no caffeine in it?"*

"Yes," I replied, *"that's exactly the point they are trying to subtly get across."*

My husband was still in shock., *"But that can't be true because I feel I have been waking up every morning with that first cup of coffee, just like they say on the Maxwell House commercial."*

I tried to let him know that, number one, he had been watching way too many commercials, and number two, it was the vitamins he was taking in the morning with that cup of coffee that were energizing his mornings. I was trying to convince him that it was all in his mind, and he should just continue with his day as usual, but I don't think he believed me. With this discussion still going on, I went about my daily routine while he refused to drink his coffee now that he felt he had been gypped of his fantasy caffeine high.

I proceeded to do what I do every morning and give my rose bushes the coffee grounds so they grow a little better. I really don't know what the purpose is or how it works, I just read about it in a book one day and started doing it. Anyway, the reason I don't think my husband bought what I was telling him about it all being in his mind stemmed from the response he gave me when I started giving the roses the coffee grounds, *"I don't know what you're doing that for, if I am not going to wake up in the morning anymore I don't know what makes you think they are going to perk up either with that decaffeinated stuff."*

"Shhhh," I replied, *"Just like you, if they don't know, then they will wake up just fine too- at least until they decide to read for the first time in their lives."*

Now, if he hadn't read the coffee can, he would still think he was waking up from that first cup of coffee. Sometimes it is better to be a mushroom in the dark than a cactus in the daylight. It's all in how you see things. If he had stayed the mushroom, he would have been fine, but he had to stick his pointed branches out to see what was going on, and he found out something he didn't like. You see how it works now?

Speaking of being in the dark, after one of the many hurricanes we had here in Florida this year we were driving around trying to see what was open to get something hot to eat. We passed a *Burger King* with a sign out front that said, "Closed due to loss of power." I was trying to figure out how this could be. The commercials specifically state that each and every one of their burgers is flame-broiled. Where do you need power for this? All you need is some wood or charcoal, lighter fluid, and a match. Then I remembered the young employees working there would be unable to give back change without the computers telling them how much to give back, so this made more sense on why they were closed.

Just to let you know, driving around in all of this is quiet dangerous with all the traffic lights hanging down and power lines on the ground. If you look at the fact we were cooped up in the house for three days without power or air, it was time to get out and see whatever we could see without walls around it. Sometimes you just need to get away, no matter what is going on. You just need a break.

While we are on the subject of getting away for a break, let's take a good look at the transportation we have for another one of our eye-openers. I'm not sure what exactly the safest transportation is but I don't think it would be flying. The way I see it is if they have to put you so far up in the air they need to give you a pressurized cabin with oxygen pumped in so you can breathe while you are flying to your destination, this is automatically a problem. If anything complicates this aircraft's cabin pressure, all thoughts of survival are out the window, and the possibility of crashing is great.

I know they will make you think everything is fine, and that all you have to do is put one of those little oxygen masks on that drop from the compartment above you. This is because they expect you to stay awake the whole time you're getting closer to the ground. My first thought is, *"Why?"* Keep in mind there is no other way out of this plane, not even a parachute. Personally I would like to be chloroformed, just enough to put me out for the panic time in that little oxygen mask; then, when I wake up – if I have lived through this, - it will be a surprise. If I don't, then that will be a surprise too.

While we are on this wild ride, put me in third class, as close to the ass-end of the plane as you can get me. From what I have seen on TV when a plane crashes it's always nose first, so if we are going to hit the ground I would like to be the last one. The way I see it, if you sit in first class you get it right after the pilots get it. Second class comes next, and then there's the ass of the plane where you could possibly have a chance to survive. Who knows, with the chloroform and sitting in the back of the plane being limp and knocked out, you might be able to bounce right out and possibly live, instead of being awakened hyperventilating with that oxygen mask on, all stiff and stressed out watching everything come to an end.

Okay, that's a little farfetched, but just think of all the other perfect opportunities of knocking out your clients for air travel with chloroform. There would be no nasty complaints, demanding assholes to drive you crazy, or drunks pinching your ass as you walk by. The terrorist population would drop dramatically. Who can hijack a plane while sleeping? You wouldn't have to feed anyone. Jet lag wouldn't be an issue either, and the staff on the plane could pick the entertainment they would like to see for their flight.

These are some good points, even though I personally still would not fly. It's too high off the ground for me. Even though I am a little overweight and I might bounce pretty safely out of the back of the plane, I certainly don't want to try it. I only like going to the airport so I can ride the tram and see all the nifty shops they have. Unfortunately, the only time I can do that is when I take someone to the airport or when I pick him or her up. Other than that I wouldn't go near an airplane.

My last visit to the airport involved picking up my mother, and sadly it was not the field trip I was hoping it would be. Because we don't put people to sleep on our planes and some people have not been kind to others, I had to get to the airport early enough to get through the pinching, poking and prodding of security to pick up my mother. Make sure you have no key chains that could be questionable, like that small cardboard finger nail file. Needless to say, after all that I was at the gate in plenty of time to watch everyone on the plane get off, right down to the pilot and stewardesses, until eventually no one else was coming down the little hallway.

There was a lady at the desk where they make the boarding announcement, so I asked her if there was a possibility that anyone else was on this plane. She says in her very professional way without looking up, *"Nope, once the staff comes off the plane it's not likely there are any more passengers on the plane."*

Trying not to disturb her as she filed her fingernails, I asked, *"What do you do if the person you were there to pick up is missing and you don't know if they got on the wrong plane?"*

In the back of my head I'm only thinking of my mother and that memory of hers. Who knows? So the busy lady behind the desk tells me I should take my concerns down to baggage claims and let them know who you are looking for. On the way to baggage claim I am thinking that this is a very odd place to send me for a person I was to pick up who never got off the plane. Do they actually think she shipped herself in her suitcase? Or worse yet, has she passed away and they just sent her in a body bag home? After pondering this I get to the baggage claim, only to stand in line with people who have lost their luggage. When I get to the clerk, he asks me for a baggage claim number. Now I am really worried. I politely begin to tell him I don't have one, I am only there to find out if my mother was possibly put on another plane. He looks up at me and says, *"Was she alive?"*

I said, *"As far as I know I put her on the plane alive to Ohio and my Aunt put her back on the plane to Florida to arrive alive. Unless there was some great surprise on the plane that I know nothing about, in which case maybe I would need that baggage claim number."*

He laughs and assures me that she was not in a body bag and sends me off to the airline terminal clerk to find my mother, since she appears to still be alive and she is not considered baggage at this time. Little does he know my husband would be in disagreement with the clerk over this, considering his pet name for her is "The Old Bag".

When I get to the airline clerk, I find out, after wandering from one end of the airport to the other for the last two and a half hours trying to find out what they have done with my mother, that they have put her on another plane because she missed her connecting flight, and she will be coming in on the next flight at 1:30am. Mind you, I have been at the airport since 9:30pm for a plane that showed up thirty minutes late without my mother on it. By the time she arrived I was tired and worn out, so when I saw my mother I was naturally cranky and I let her know she was now grounded from traveling alone without one of her adult daughters' for supervision.

Yes, becoming the adult child entitles you to grounding the parent at any given time when she seems to be reverting to the teenage years of no brakes. This seems to have cured her from traveling. She hasn't been back on a plane since, nor has she traveled alone. She always takes one of my sisters with her or me. As a result of the ordeal I went though for four hours, I don't want to go to another airport ever again, even for shopping or riding the tram. I think at this stage of the game I would prefer a boat, and there are plenty of shops on them. There are also many more options to save your life, un-less, of course, you were on the Titanic path in icy cold-water. Then one option in this life saving effort wouldn't work, and that would be the life preserver.

Look at the possibilities of being on a cruise. You get a little boat if the big one sinks and if the little one doesn't do well, you get an inflatable little boat to float in. Last, but not least, if all else fails, you have a life preserver. You get life preservers on the plane, too, but I'm not sure how you'd get out of the plane to use it if you went down under the water. Unless the tail end of the plane breaks off before it sinks, and then my theory of sitting in the back of the plane would work again.

The boat deal seems to have better planning, don't you think? I look at the boat for a relaxing way to travel and the plane for a fast and possibly stressful way to travel. I'd rather be relaxed. It's kind of like the **"JAWS"** effect; you don't want to go swimming in the ocean any longer than you absolutely have to and you will think of the other possibilities than a plane ride or a boat ride to travel to your vacation destinations.

There are other means to get around like driving your car, riding the bus or the train. All three of these land transports could be considered a better, safer way of traveling. Although the bus seems like a fairly good idea because someone else is driving you, the truth of that matter is you may not like the company that sits so close to you. What about the fact that they make so many stops to drop off and pick up that you get there five, ten, twenty hours longer than what it would have taken for you to drive yourself. Then you find yourself sitting on this bus watching the signs go by, *stop in and see the world's largest fireworks shop*, or *come experience White Waterfalls next exit.*

If you drive yourself, you can stop wherever the hell you want. I have always wanted to see a sign like this one when I was traveling, *"Stop in and see the world's largest asshole."* I guess if that were an option, there would be a lot of signs out there.

Men would retaliate with, *"Look at the bitch I live with."*

We would probably end up with more billboards on the road than cars and have to blindfold our children for the trip.

Anyway, back to this transportation issue of the bus. The other problem with this is what happens if you get a driver who hasn't had enough sleep, and he starts snoring at the wheel? You don't have co-pilots to take over who could nudge him to get up. *"Hey, buddy! Wake up! The road was put in for us to drive on, not for us to watch it pass by while you chase the cows in the pasture."* There is the bus experience.

The train is all right, I guess. I haven't had experience on a train. I don't think I would like to watch the scenery go by at 100 miles an hour. I would definitely be train-sick. I have a hard enough time sitting in my car watching the trains go by as I'm sitting still. My eyes get tired and dizzy, my stomach get queasy. I want to go home and get back in bed.

I drive my car everywhere I want to go. I figure if I can't get there by boat or my car, I don't need to go. But after being in a rear-end car accident this year, I am beginning to wonder if even it is safe. I have always bought big-ass cars thinking I was safe and I couldn't get hurt in them. My thinking was that any of the fiberglass wonders, as I so generously call all these new cars they have built, could hit me and nothing would happen to my car, but their car would be totaled. This set-up works, only if the trunk isn't rusted out, which I didn't know mine was until after the fact. My car had a dent on the roof in the middle of the car, which was an indication of the frame being bent. I was right about one thing - the little girl who hit me, with one of the new Suzuki jeeps or trucks. Whatever it was didn't look as if it had an ounce of damage, but the entire under carriage of the vehicle - motor and transmission – was hanging out from underneath. The rubber stuff bounced back, but the plastic stuff holding the metal pieces in place gave out.

The insurance company sent a tow-truck driver to pick up my car. I noticed he had a little Suzuki on the back that looked like the one that had hit me. So I asked him if that was the vehicle and he replied yes. He then proceeded to tell me what was wrong with the vehicle and that they had totaled hers out, too.

It's amazing to me how well they used to build cars in the 40's, 50's,60's, and 70's, with the cost being an incredible $300- $5000. Compare that to now, where everything is made out of thin metal – so thin I often think it might be where all of our re-cycled soda cans go. Our recycled milk jugs are now our plastic bumpers. You have to take out a second mortgage just to afford the car, and you don't even live, sleep, shower or pee in the thing. It's the disposable car that you will have to throw away in two years, provided you don't get hit. Then it could be sooner.

I once had a kid come up to me with a little Honda and tell me that his car was going to be a classic just like the "old school cars" you see now. I thought to myself there wouldn't be much of that car left. The plastic bumpers would crack and disin-tegrate. The motor would have been replaced at least 20 times in 30 years, and every bolt in that car would have been shaken loose by the "boom boom boom" of the music played in it. If the poor car could make it though all of this, the kid would be in debt 'till he was sixty as a result of the cost of the parts he'd need just to keep it in like-new condition.

The cost of electronics is astounding when it comes to these new vehicles, and the prices you have to pay to change parts. I see all these ads to buy a new car and they all say the same thing, *"Now is the time to buy a new car."* I wonder when would be a bad time. Is it Friday, when all the workers at the factory building the car have the five o'clock whistle on their minds, so their minds are not on what they are putting in your car? They have more to think about -like going out and having a good time with their friends at the bar after work, and this thought started when they walked into work that morning and punched the clock. So how well do you think your car is being put together on this day?

Or would it be bad to buy a car built the Monday when the workers return after having a good time for the weekend, hung-over and suffering from lack of sleep. I can only imagine what quality of work you're getting; lights that go off when they feel like it, mis-spelled warnings on the information screen in the car, *"ARNING LO FUL"*, or the idiot light that comes on and actually says. *"IDIOT"*. How about that window that just crashes down in the door when you hit a bump driving the car off the lot, or maybe the window that won't go down at all but you can hear the motor running.

The best ad I have heard so far is about the Ford Focus. It says, *"Let the power of the Ford Focus throw you back into your seat."* I couldn't help myself. I started laughing so hard I had tears coming from my eyes. How in the hell is a four-cylinder car going to throw you back in your seat? There was only one thing I could think of that would throw you back in your seat and that would be the electronic seat belt coming across your chest as you put the car's shifter into the drive position. The other part that gets me is that all of this is happening while you still have your foot on the brake and you haven't made it off the car lot yet.

I would rather have a car from the 60's or 70's that would only have necessities that are needed to run the car and really throw you back into your seat without a seat belt; a motor, transmission, alternator, and a battery, all the easy things that can be fixed without a mechanic with an engineering/electrical degree. This would give the backyard mechanic a chance at a living too. Just the basics, no frills or fancy seats and gadgets in the car that will costume an arm and a leg to replace.

I do own a 1972 Dodge Charger with a 440 engine and I wouldn't trade it for the world. The regulator for this car—this is the piece that helps it start—was $2.98. This definitely beats the $150.00 I paid for a regulator for the '95 Lincoln I had. Had is the key word there because I traded it in for a 1979 Cadillac El Doraderado, something less expensive to fix and pay for.

I have always tried to live life simply. If you try to have everything before you die, I feel you will die early from all the stress and pressure you create to have it all. I don't believe in keeping up with the Joneses. I feel if I'm meant to have it all, I will, and if not, I won't. Having a good time while I'm here on earth is all I want to do. I work to pay my bills that are within a budget. Nothing over that or I will not be able to do any other fun things like go to the beach, the zoo, or the festivals for whatever season is here. I work to play, not to pay all my life.

Have you ever wondered where some sayings and expression came from? I just came up with the work to pay but where do some of the odd ones come from like, *"I hope you didn't pay an arm and a leg for that."* It makes me wonder if someone in the past actually had to do that. *"Give me your arm for those goods you just bought, sir".* I know it sounds ridiculous, but some expressions do come from past generations that just don't make a lick of sense to me like, *"dumber than a box of rocks."* When did they become a living organism?

"That's enough to aggravate the balls right off a pool table." You're on your own for that one. I have no clue.

"She's a few sandwiches short of a picnic basket." This, I guess, is a nice way to say she is stupid.

"My nose itches. Someone must be come to see me with holes in their britches." (This was something from the hillbillies' book of *"Buford's Predictions"* no doubt.)

Most of these are still used to this day and a few new ones have been discovered with the *"yo momma"* sayings like, *"Yo momma is so dumb she tries to put M&Ms in alphabetical order."* And the picnic basket has been upgraded to dry-wall, as in: *"He's long on dry-all, short on studs."* The one that took me the longest time to get was, *"Man, she's phat."* My teenage daughter had to explain to me that this does not mean overly big. It means she looks good.

My grandmother, I thought, had the best saying when she was angry with my grandfather. She had a great sense of humor, like me. It went something like this, *"The Lord brought you to me and he can take you back."* Some of these are really weird huh?

Speaking of weird - from past to weird present - there was a situation at work the other day with someone graduating from one of our programs with the last name Dickgrabber. No, I am not stretching the truth or pulling your leg, the client's last name was really Dickgrabber. Everyone at work was laughing and thinking we would have changed that last name when we were old enough to know what it meant. During this thought process, one of our co-workers stated that this was not that funny and she went on to say, *"Maybe it was a name of a trade back in the 1700's. You know a lot of last names were taken from the trade you were skilled in."*

This had me laughing to the point where I had tears running down my face, and I couldn't breathe. All I could think was, *"This would have been considered a trade?"* Were people actually running around grabbing any dick they could get their hands on?

During all of this laughter, another co-worker stepped up and he had yet more words of wisdom on this subject: *"It could have been a tradesman name like "Deckgrabber"-a Decksman on a boat - and somehow, over time, the name was changed a little."*

A little? This made my mind run in another direction, which made me unable to stop laughing, and now I was ready to pee in my pants. Here's what I was playing in my head: *One of the actors from the movie "THEBIRDCAGE" - Robin Williams or Nathan Lane -on a ship in the 1700's sail-*

ing around the world with men running up and down the ship pulling the hoists for the sails as he's running around grabbing the other decksmen's dicks saying, "fossy, fossy one fossy fossy two." And this is how the deckgrabber became a dick-grabber by the time they reached the next port.

This to me was very humorous; where there is opportunity for humor to be introduced, my mind will find it and put it into action. There was a time that I had sold all my vacation time for my daughter and her boyfriend to get into their first apartment. Yes, I try to do all I can for my children and selling my vacation was fine. I didn't figure I would be able to afford to go anywhere that year, so why not give the kids their first apartment? After they were finished moving in, they invited me for dinner. My daughter's boyfriend thanked me for helping them out so much. He said if there was anything he could do to help me one day to just let him know.

With that I stated, *"You are very welcome but just remember this: When I need a vacation, I will be coming here, lying by the pool while you serve me fruity drinks with little umbrellas in them while I*

make fancy postcards from my computer for every-
one at work to think I am somewhere exotic."

This he found very funny and agreed to serve
me my drinks, provided it was on his day off from
one of his two jobs. My daughter's boyfriend is
very humorous himself when it comes to getting the
little things in life. He and my daughter received
their gym room key for the apartment they were living in. My daughter calls me the next day to ask me
something, probably to barrow money, but can't
even breathe or talk, she is laughing so hard. She
finally gets around to telling me what it is that is
making her laugh so hard. Her boyfriend had just
gotten back from his first workout at the gym and
proceeded to take a shower to clean up. When he
got out of the shower he was parading around the
house naked doing the Mr. Universe poses and saying *"I'm going to be buff, I'm going to be buff, I*
might end up with a little pecker but I'm going to be
buff."

Needless to say, I was laughing hysterically,
too. It reminded me of a few weeks before when I
put my husband in a bubble bath to relax after a

long hard day at work. I walk into bring him a towel and I found him playing with the bubbles saying, *"I'm going to be sthilky sthoft."*.

This was funny. It reminded me of a little boy playing with toys in the bathtub and having a good time. I really don't think men ever grow up. If they get close enough, they hit mid-life crisis, and then they go through puberty all over again. I'm sure you've seen them out there during this stage, wearing the younger generations clothes, driving the two-seated convertible sports cars with the 2x4's they just purchased from the home improvement store in the passenger seat.

Just like men, we women go through some changes of our own but for some reason it is done in stages every month rather than every year, and I read this in one of my many e-mails: *A study at the University of Missouri Medical School shows that the type of men's facial features that a woman finds attractive can differ, depending upon where she is in her cycle. For example: most of the month a woman is attracted to men with kind, smooth, clean-shaven features. If she is ovulating, she is attracted to men with rugged and masculine features. During her period or if she is menopausal, she is more prone to be attracted to a man with scissors shoved in his temple and a bat jammed up his ass while he is on fire.*

When I read this I was thinking to myself that this is really true. There are days I love my husband and think about him all day the same way I did when we first met. Then there are days I can't stand the sight or the sound of him. I feel these emotions intensify in women when you are nine months pregnant. My first husband and I had a waterbed and I just could not get out of it without help when I was at the last stages of my pregnancy. There was a night I just couldn't stand his being near me or even hearing him snore, but I couldn't roll out of that waterbed to save my life. The bumpers kept bumping me back in. This made me even more frustrated, because I now knew what a beached whale felt like.

His snoring was driving me crazy, so I resorted to stuffing two of my fingers up his nose to cut off the noisemaker that way. As he woke up, I quickly took my fingers out and just lay there as if nothing was going on. He jumped up, looking around, and said, *"I dreamt I couldn't breathe."*

"Really?" I said, *"How awful that must have been,"* knowing the whole time that I was the root of this problem that was going to keep him up for the rest of the night, which was good for me because I didn't have to lie next to him, see him, or hear him snore again for the rest of the night.

The next morning I woke up and loved to be around him again.

Sometimes there doesn't have to be an opportunity like that for something funny to pop into your head, just the wondering and thought process of trying to figure out why, how, or what for could have you stumbling upon something humorous. Example: There was a documentary on TV one time about white supremacy groups and how they thought about most of the world and other races and religions. This was a disturbing show for me at first, but I, of course, started to ask why, wondering where this hostility could possibly come from, and I found some humor in this organization that felt so strongly about themselves. The first thought that I found humor in was the question, *what happens to-tem when they pass away and go to heaven? What would happen if they went to confess their sins in front of God, and to their surprise God just happens to be... Whoopi Goldberg?*

Now my question is, *do they stay or just opt for going to hell and take their chances on who's there? Dean Martin and Sammy Davis Jr. together again singing in Italian.*

I have never understood these groups that point out their differences to the rest of the world thinking they are better than others. We all have the same problems and stresses in life. Go to work, pay the bills, and try to better yourself or help your kids have something better than you. Or, on the other end of the spectrum, we all commit crimes so we don't have to work - stealing, selling drugs, etc. Regardless of what we do in life, we all bleed the same color when we get cut, so unless you see some green or purple blood coming out, why have problems with anyone at all.

Take a minute to think about this. Men and women have been sluts since the beginning of time, sleeping with anyone, no matter what religion, race, or ethnic background. They've had children they don't even know about while traipsing around the world discovering new lands, and you're going to create a group or organization because you just happened to come out with brown eyes when everyone else has blue? Please, get off the cross, honey. Someone else could use the wood.

Who puts this stuff in their heads without looking at the big picture? It's just plain ignorance, and in this case I found some humor rather than being angry.

There are lots of things you see in this world that make you go "hmumm." One is, who the hell thought to put **"DO NOT PUSH"** on the back of a dump truck without instructions? I pictured two rednecks with a dump truck almost to the top of a hill that has broke down. There is one in the truck with his hand on the emergency brake release handle and the other at the back of the truck with his back braced against back of the truck and his arms behind him on the bumper. With this in mind I hear the one holding on to the back of the truck saying,

"Okay, Buford, you can go ahead and pull that emergency brake, and let's see if I can git her up over the hill".

This was my definition to the Do Not Push. I now know that this is not the correct meaning. It was put there so you don't ride their ass.

It's amazing what your mind can come up with while sitting in traffic for one or two hours after a hard day's work. Let me give you a little warning on obstructing traffic during a busy time of day. I had a spider in my car once; you know, one the size of a baseball, and it crawled on my leg at a stoplight so I swatted it off, put the car in park and got out. Two cars back was a police officer who pulled up wanting to know why I got out of my car, and if I had plans to get back in the car any time soon because the light was green. I needed to just get in my car and move on. I explained that I was not getting in the car with the spider so the officer then proceeded to get into the car and killed the spider with his clipboard. After all this, he wrote me a ticket for obstructing traffic to which I replied, *"$25.00? That's an expensive extermination, don't you think?*

If I have to pay this ticket, the least you could do is be a good exterminator and take the carcass out of the car."

I was in luck. He got a paper towel out of his car and took the dead spider out of my car. This I am sure was the talk of the station that day. I would like to think I gave the officer a little humor for the day as he gave me peace of mind by taking the dead spider out of the car so that it wouldn't be a *Stephen King* moment, and it couldn't suddenly come back to life and get me another $25.00 ticket.

Sometimes there are people out there with a sense of humor that can bring you a good laugh when you are at the end of your rope. My husband has a friend who helped him laugh a little during a time in his business that the county was driving him crazy with all the changes. He had to do all kinds of new things for his licensing one year because the city we lived in wanted to make it tougher for businesses that didn't know what they were doing to get a license. It was unfortunate for those who knew what they were doing for the last five, ten, twenty years. The city was making them miserable. To make a long story short, he had to have reference letters from three clients, so he asked three that he had done work for recently and one of them was a gentleman he had become friends with who had a wonderful way of de-stressing situations. He decided to make his first letter not much of a reference but more of a gag letter, giving my husband a good laugh, which he desperately needed with as much stress as he was under at this time. This was what the letter stated:

To Whom It May Concern: I have known Jason Kismoky for a few years now. I really don't know him that much. However when I was doing a two-year stretch of hard labor in a naval brig, I met a lot of nice guys just like him. Maybe it's the prison tattoos he's got that remind me of them. Jason did some tile work for us when we first met. Although the work was pretty shoddy, the price was right. He explained to me that if I paid him cash instead of by check, he wouldn't have to declare it to the I.R.S., so you can see he is a good businessman. On one occasion last year. our home was broken into. He offered to take my wife with him to buy glass to help me out by fixing our broken window. Five hours later, they both returned in a joyous mood and gave me his receipt from Motel 6 where he claims they were selling windows cheap. Now I ask you, where you can find a friend like that? I think he deserves his license renewed for one reason or another, I guess? Sincerely, Anonymous

This letter is exactly what I have been talking about; throughout life's little ups and downs, we need desperately to find some humor in it. I see other people's sense of humor sometimes in sales ads or people advertising to gain your attention and get you curious enough to either call or go by to look at what they have. My husband and I drove 300 miles just to look at a car because of the advertising.

Sale: Pontiac Firebird Esprit Sale

I bought this car at Jim Moran Pontiac in Hollywood on Aug. 2, 1977, for my wife. She has cared for it like a baby and I've done what I can to keep it running, which hasn't always been a picnic; However; it still goes up and down the road and looks damn good doing it. Having been parked in a garage all its life certainly helped, but the excellent

Deltron 2000 paint with clear coat applied in 1994 did wonders for her beauty restoration. Didn't make her run any better, but she looks real good trying. I can't recall ever driving her on a trip. One time to Ocala and back by my wife, but mostly a very sheltered life, going to Public school and the mall. Now we must part. I'm too old to fix her and can't afford to pay others to do it. She is not reliable enough and requires too much coddling for us Medicare folks. You can be her next proud owner for around 5k. Your final cost will depend on whether or not I think you will treat her right. Could be more, could be less. It's more important I find her a good home than the $ I receive for her adoption. Please call me first on the cell. If unable there, try the home, but be warned...should you reach my wife at home you may experience weeping and wailing. She will beg you not to buy the car. Ignore her and call me.

We did try calling the house once just to see if his wife would talk us out of buying the car, but all we heard was, *"Jim, dear, the phone."* The weeping and wailing must come when someone actually buys the car and it leaves the driveway.

Five thousand was a little much for a car that needed mechanical work and some body work. The car was maybe worth three thousand tops. We hadn't intended to spend that much on a car that needed a lot of work anyway, but we had to go see what it looked like and what kind of people they were to think of such a cleaver add.

I think has all people have a little humor in them. They just need to let it loose once in a while. I once threw a trashcan to the curb to be picked up because it had a hole in it and was cracked down the side, so it was time to retire it. To insure that the trash men would not just empty it and leave it for me to take out next week, I placed a nice sign on it:

Hi! I am retiring today. I have served my own-ers well the last few years. Come rain or shine or the idiot across the street hitting me every now and then, I always came out full of goodies with every intention of coming back empty to get filled up again and go back out next week. But alas, the idiot has hit me too many times and hurricane Erin didn't help by lowering a tree branch on me, so here I am for you to take me to my final resting place. You have a wonderful day. Sincerely, Retired Trash Can.

I watched the trash men pick up that day, and I saw them smiling and laughing. One even put the note in his pocket. He probably took it home and framed it. I would have.

I have one more that I wrote for a classic car my husband bought to fix up and resell that we wound up getting attached to, so we named her and gave her the best ad of any other vehicle being sold. Here is her debut in the classic car section.

Hi! My name is Myrtle; I am a 1973 Ford Grand Torino, and unlike traditional breakdowns of my Ford name found on the road dead or fixed or repaired daily, I am a Foxy Old Rare Dame. I have only 72,000 original miles with a tight motor that purrs like a kitten. I have a body like Farrah Fawcet, and my curves of yesterday are most sought after today. My Measurements are 302, C4, 8"411 Posi rear end, with my rear end being the main attraction. Even at 31 years young, I can run circles around the younger generation because I was built to last. Just look at my nearly perfect interior, fac-

tory floor mats and four new booties. I'm a good catch for $3000.00. If you're interested, talk to these good owners of mine. Sincerely, Myrtle.

I think I should make myself a business out of this called *"Catchy Slogans by Michelle...Make anything you have a Star"*. What do ya think?

At least I make signs that make you laugh at, not wonder what I meant when I wrote it. I was traveling on the other side of Florida in Clearwater when I came upon a sign in front of a restaurant that said, *"Now open to the public."* What does this mean? Who were they open to before?

Everywhere I go it seems that I can find humor in anything, and sometimes humorous people like me just put it on a sign in front of their work. The church I pass every day on my way to work always has such nice sayings on its sign, usually wisdom from the Bible. One day I passed by and the sign said, *"Don't let the hearse be the first one to take you to church."* I giggled all the way to work.

CHAPTER FIVE

Generation "F"

Is this where the next generation of people may be heading to? What ever happen to *Ladies and Gentlemen?* Are we becoming extinct?

Where there used to be Mr. and Mrs. Smith, now it's, *"I would like to introduce you to Mr. and Mrs. Foul Mouth, and their children Shit, Damn, Fuck, and Bitch will be here any day now".*

I know as a woman I am happy to have equal rights and all, but I'm not sure I would like to sign up for the swearing contest between men and women. I wonder how sexy a guy thinks a woman is that says the "F" word every other sentence or vice versa. This word seems to be very versatile in that is used as a noun, verb, adverb, adjective and pronoun. Swearing seems to be our new language used to greet, introduce, lead, and end a conversation with. When did "Bitch" and "Dog" become a positive greeting for someone? Why is Yo used to tell someone hello? Are they not being taught enough in school, because they seem to be missing some letters or words when they talk or write? *Watz up. How r u? My BFF.*

How do you show up to special events or even Christmas shop in public with them? Well, for one thing they probably wouldn't be invited to a special event that would require suits and dresses. At least not yet give it a few more generations; by then everyone will be dressing down and dressing up in a suit or dress will become optional. How did we get here? How did we get to where the men wear clothes three times too big and the women wear clothes three times too small?

Dressing up for a man these days is their pants falling down to show off their underwear, and we are thankful that there is new underwear. And shoes are to be worn untied. Especially work boots that have nothing to do with work.

For women, dressing up is a loin cloth that just barely covers the goodies and adding the highest heels to the outfit. I'm not sure if you're dressed for a night out on the town or you're getting ready to work the nearest street corner in town. What happen to women? They are nowhere near lady-like any more. In fact, they seem to have more testosterone then men, with the way their tempers fly off the handle and they are ready to start a fight at the drop of a hat. They swear like sailors whether talking to their friends in the store shopping or on the cell phone talking to a friend. This didn't used to happen until women were going through menopause and couldn't figure out why they were taking the spatula and killing the over-easy eggs in the frying pan for no reason. Swear words would only come out by accident and when they did. you apologized for using it.

Men used to bring flowers home to the one they loved. Now it's *"nothing says romance like a Red Dirt Devil vacuum cleaner."*

This was my gift this year from my husband for Valentine's Day. Is it just me or am I not the only one who would have rather had the red roses?

My daughter, who is twenty-four years old has a hard time with dating men her age. She continuously tells me they don't listen to how she feels or what she wants. Granted, I love my daughter with all my heart, but she herself is not listening to them, either. This generation has become selfish in only thinking about themselves and not what they can do for others. My daughter doesn't see her own short-comings but feels she is going to find Prince Charming.

I have explained to her that the only man who will listen to how she feels and understand it enough to give feed-back is a gay man, which means you will have to give up sex for more intellectual conversations about yourself. As for Prince Charming, I told her she would have to go to Disney World to find him, but just remember, once the costume comes off, he will be just like any other guy.

She doesn't have the concept that a relationship is for two people to work together and compromising is essential to make it work. But I guess the men she is dating doesn't understand that either. The whole generation seems to think it is either their way or the highway.

I realize that we have gone though some really big changes here and that every generation has a signature thing about them. We live in a world that with each generation new ideas, morals and values have come along. Not necessarily what was taught to us from our parents or to our parents from their parents.

I also realize that we as women have always fought for equal rights which were great to be able to do everything men do, but did we have to lose our femininity? For example, I was taught everyone is a person no matter what shape, color, or planet they may be from and they all get treated with respect. You can agree to disagree tactfully, not with a good fist fight. When you leave the house, make sure you are dressed with self-confidence and presentable in case you run in to someone important. This didn't mean put make-up on my face and run out the door in my pajama bottoms, a tank-top with no bra, and a pair of slippers.

My husband, on the other hand, was taught keep his hair combed back, dress appropriately and treat people with respect; but don't trust anyone. Even though the money says *"In God we trust,"* don't.

That reminds me of when my husband was trying to figure out God and how all of it works. My husband had a hard time believing in God, but this was how his parents raised him. He was having a terrible time with a man that came to our house often, pestering him for beer and wanting him to get drunk with him all the time. This was annoying him something terrible. The man would come over all hours of the day and night, *"Hey, man, let's have a few drinks together"*. All this and he never brought an ounce of alcohol with him.

We tried telling him we didn't have any a couple of times but then he got smart and started showing up when we came from the grocery store. My husband finally had enough and told the guy to never come back to the house again. He then sits by the phone waiting for it to ring. I asked him, *"Ho-*

ney, who are you expecting to get a call from?"

He said, *"You know, the man upstairs."*

Mind you, we do not have a two-story house so I assumed he was waiting on God to call. *"Why are you waiting for God to call?"*

He replied, *"Because I did a good thing by getting rid of the bad guy."*

I explained it didn't work that way, and he just needed to be happy with his decision and know God would be proud of him just like his parents would be when you make the right choices in life. A few days went by and I had checked the phone to see what calls had been missed that day while I was out. Oddly enough on the caller ID it said, *House of God Miami.* I gave my husband the phone to and said, *"Look, God called and he is here in Florida on vacation in Miami. You could call him back and see what he wants."*

My husband quickly replies, *"I have no beef with that man, I don't need to call him back. Everything is fine."*

I laughed.

That Sunday we passed the church on our way to my sister's house. The Pastor was outside on his cell phone and all the parishioners were in the church. My husband asked, *"Who do you think he is talking to?"*

I looked at him and said, *"Probably God to see if he likes the sermon he has selected for the day. He probably found out God was in Miami on vacation so he decided to give him a call and see what he thought of his sermon for the day."*

My husband just looked at me and said, *"You're funny. You really think he's calling him?"*

I was reading the paper the other day and saw a headline that was interesting; 'God" was arrested near Tampa church. The article read, *Police say a man named God was arrested near a Tampa church for selling cocaine. Authorities began investigating God Lucky Howard in April, and he was arrested on Saturday. Police say he sold the cocaine to undercover detectives in his neighborhood. When officers searched his home, they reported finding another 22 grams of cocaine and a scale. Jail records show Howard was charged with several counts drug possession and distribution, which include increased charges for being within 1,000 feet of a church, a school and public housing.*

Now after reading this a lot of things went through my head like, *what were his parents on when they named him?*

Because they don't give his age, I was just wondering if he was a product of the 60's where everyone had these unusual names for their children while expanding their minds. Was it supposed to be *Got Lucky Howard* and the parents were so far out there that they misspelled '*got*'?

There are some very unusual names out there, you know, like Moon Zappa, Rainbow Trout, Harry Sacks, and Molten Glasscock. These are just to name a few. Judging by their last names, I think the parents were either trying to make some kind of a statement or they were high and thought this was funny. While researching these names on the internet, I found a recent article for New Zealand where the parents were fighting with officials over the name of their newborn. They intended to name him 4Real but because there was a number in front of the name the officials were not going to allow it, so the parents changed the name to Superman. Tell me I am not the only one that is wondering, *"What"?* This just proves there are good drugs all over the world and there are a lot of people on them. There just doesn't seem to be clear thinking involved here.

The same day I read about God being arrested I also read about a man that calls 9-1-1 after being robbed of 12,000 dollars while trying to purchase 20 pounds of marijuana. I want to know how much marijuana he smoked before going to purchase more of this illegal drug and was robbed. I am just wondering what part of his brain was functioning when he decided to call the police about it. You are trying to purchase an illegal drug, you get robbed, somewhere inside that brain of yours you convince yourself you won't get in trouble because you didn't actually get the dope, so it should be ok to call the police and try to at least get your money back. It is like the man calling from a pay-phone for an ambulance in Tennessee having trouble breathing and needs help now. When the dispatcher asks him where he is he gives the address and the dispatcher tells him help is on the way. The dispatcher then asks what he was doing before he had complications breathing, the man replies, *running from the cops.*

Now who do you think is going to show up with the ambulance? I know what you're thinking about some of those clichés about the northern mountain folks but let's just say for the heck of it this man was not naïve nor missing some tools in the tool shed in any way, so what would have possessed him to tell the truth? My first guess would be moon shine and my second would be some type of drug.

Somewhere along the way this must be some type of excitement for them or the thrill of the chase and hopefully not getting caught. I guess it was more the thrill of the chase for most because they did get caught.

You know there used to be a time when 'suspenseful' was seeing what kind of trouble the Beaver was going to get into next on *Leave it to Beaver* or what Marsha was devastated over on the *Brady Bunch*. The detective shows like *Dragnet* and *Car*

54 where when people got shot you never saw the blood gushing out, just a circular tear in the shirt where the bullet supposedly went in. Most of the people getting arrested would either give up gracefully or run down the road a piece and finally just turn around and put their hand behind their backs to be cuffed.

People used words like *"book'em, Dano"*, *"gosh darned"*, *"holy cow"*, *"shoot"* and maybe the occasional, *"damn."* Now a days, the more guts showing, the more blood bath the show becomes, the better they like it. When you go to see a movie if you don't come out of the movie theater with the paranoia that someone is waiting to get you in the parking lot, a pee stain on the front of you and popcorn and soda on your head from the people behind you, that was not a good movie. The more cussing bloodshed and internal body parts exposed or, if in 3D, landing in your lap, the better. It's like Halloween all year long.

Video games are the same; the only difference is you are actually involved in the killings of people who look real and talk like the "F" generation. Which is scary if you think about how our society has become so angry and violent towards everything. It's almost as if we are giving them practice sessions at the gun range only instead of the paper target we have the likeness of real people on our private television screens at home.

The most violent game I played as a kid was Pac Man and Galaxian. A tennis ball chewing the ghost up wasn't bad because they always came back to get you. Shooting fictional alien ships was ok because they always came back in round two but the best part was these characters didn't exist in real life. It wasn't like you were going to run into Mr. and Mrs. Pac Man somewhere on the street or have dinner parties with the neighbor aliens.

This generation seems to be in search of more thrills and looking at violent ways to find it. Kids used to love riding the Farris wheel or Mr. Toad's wild ride. Now they are looking for the next bad-ass roller coaster that will flip them upside down, give them whiplash and just literally scare the pants or tops right off of them. These people are trying to

keep up with death wishes and some are succeeding.

We used to try to keep up with the Jones's and
looking to see if the grass was any greener on the
other side of the fence. We were quick to find out
that the Jones's were so far in debt they were filling
for bankruptcy and would be living with relatives in
a smaller home than their shed, and the grass was
only greener because the septic tank was over-
flowing in the yard. We also found out they still
have to mow the yard and pull weeds just like
yours. So it really wasn't worth it in the end to
keep up with them.

I had a girl in one of my classes that said, *"I
will be a happy camper if everything continues to
go my way."* Meaning if everything she had set up
to be just like someone else kept going smoothly,
she would have everything they had and more.
More was definitely what she wanted because she
felt if she had more than them she was better than
they were. She asked me what I thought and the
only reply I had was, *"Do you have a spare tent for
this camping trip just in case it rains and the tent*

springs a leak?" She was frustrated with me and felt that I was bringing her happiness down. The truth was no one should be looking down at anyone else unless you have your hand out to help them up.

At least, that is how it used to be. Way back when it didn't seem like we had so many people trying to clone themselves after someone else. You admired their strength and determination and they were role models, letting you know you could do anything you wanted to do. You should have your own dreams and goals for what you want because even if you think you have everything and you think it makes you superior to someone else, if it isn't something that is truly you then the happiness won't last long and being superior I would think gets lonely.

This generation is trying so hard to be just like everyone else and not who they really are. They feel that by being a thug, male or female, and cussing in conversations they are somehow unique. If you are unique then why do you all look and sound the same as everyone else? Ask them this and it goes right over their head. They don't get it. I love it when I get the answer, *"This is who I am. I grew up in the 'hood and this is how we roll."*

We all have grown up in the hood, neighbor-**hood** and you don't see us acting a fool disrespecting everyone and everything.

I have one question, *why in world do you need a song that last fifteen minutes for your answering service on the cell phone.* By the time you listen to the whole thing, swear words being the only recognizable words on the whole recording, you have forgotten what it was you called for. What happened to, *"Hi, it's me. If that's you, leave a message"?* Short, sweet and I still use it.

It left me thinking that this may be why most young people don't have a job. What person at work has time to listen to all that. The only thing we have time to listen to is the elevator music in the elevator on the way to our desk. This generation has some grandeur idea that they will be rap stars or a successful high-end drug dealer rubbing elbows with the rich and famous people. They think they will be given a lot of money for doing nothing without any consequences. It seems everyone is caught up in the easy money scheme. You see it on TV with every lawyer in town advertising how they can get money for any accident. *Accident?* Why do we still call it that when all of them end up in lawsuits? Whatever happened to letting the insurance company fix the cars and away you go. Whiplash claims out the ass. How do you get whiplash when your head is securely nestled between the headrest and the air bag? If this is still a problem, maybe we should be looking at the movie *'Demolition Man'* where the car completely encases you in foam. Maybe when we rear-end someone, we should have a lawsuit written up instead of a ticket.

It seems as though we have become a society that very few take the time to think of someone else and what they may need. The few that are left are now on Oprah as heroes and angels. You know there is a problem when you see strong healthy men passing an elderly man broke down in the middle of the road and they have the nerve to beep their horns and yell at him to get out of the way rather than help the guy out. I had to get out of my car in a dress and high heels to help push him on to the shoulder.

Then the idiots still didn't stop, they just whistled and made comments about the heels and dress. If I can help the guy out all dressed up, what is your excuse?

Work boots are only a tax deduction for work, suit just came from the dry cleaners and you might break a sweat. Are people so wrapped up and involved with themselves they can't see past their own front door? It seems that all anyone can think about any more is, *how much money can I get and will I die before I get my million dollars?*

What ever happened to living life to its fullest, seeing the world before you die? If you wait for the million to see the world you might not get to see anything but your own back yard and work.

Speaking of dying, my mother received a card in the mail today that was a little unusual since she couldn't think of any birthdays that were coming up. She wondered who it was from and what kind of celebration was being acknowledged. When she opened it she saw a beautiful card with flowers and little butterflies on the front with the words, *"Free prepaid cremation. For more information, look inside"*.

The inside was filled with details of how you could enter the contest to win a free cremation. *Limited time only and offer expires soon.* Remember the good old days when you would enter yourself to win a car, appliances, TV or maybe even a cash prize from Ed McMahon. Granted at sixty-two years old you are thinking some day in the next twenty years your number will be up, but you would like to think you could actually win something you could have fun with or use until that time comes. Winning this prize doesn't sound like you're in for a good time. Maybe it should be a brochure making it sound like the best last vacation you will ever need. Something like this will do, I'm sure:

THE PLEASURES OF SIMPLER TIMES WHERE HISTORY LOVES COMPANY.

Come get away this year to the most popular natural wonder and family gathering that celebrities such as Greta Garbo, Cary Grant, Vivian Leigh, and Rock Hudson have embarked on. Enjoy the freedom from bills, obligation, in-laws, and all that ails you. Relax, explore, enjoy, and experience all the amenities we have to offer. You can experience one of our un-crowded two hour red hot cruises through the wonderful world of incineration. This cruise is guaranteed to help you lose all your unwanted pounds, stress and much more. When this cruise is over, you will feel as light as a feather. It will feel almost as if you could become airborne with the slightest breeze. After the cruise you will settle yourself right into a wide variety of affordable accommodations such as the rustic cabin urn, the authentic urn, or any other beautiful urn of your choice.

Just when you think your stay is over we throw you and your closest friends and family the best party in the world with an open bar and a huge buffet featuring all your favorites crab legs, lobster tails, and don't forget the seven layer chocolate cake for dessert.

Enjoy the last vacation you will ever need with us. We warmly welcome you to our land of natural beauty! No bones about it we welcome you with open urns.

FREE tours every day.

It's amazing how far we have come in the last hundred years. We have come from fun contests to ones that the requirement is death to enjoy it. I went to a women health conference this week and the two grand prizes were winning a free preparation of a last will and testament. Now I may be wrong, but I thought going to a women's health conference was to teach you how to be healthy and live longer. I was also wondering if we are looking at world extinction in 2012, who in the world would we leave anything to? Well, times have sure changed and I am not even half-way through it yet.

Everyone used to know their neighbors when I was a kid, now they avoid knowing them. Everyone is under the impression if you should happen to get to know your neighbors they all seem to end up on the news being arrested for having a grow house, meth lab or some type of child abuse. Family time way back when was six o'clock when everyone sat down to the dinner table, laughing and talking about their day. Now it's yelling at everyone trying to rush them out the door for school and work. Coming home rushing them through dinner and straight to bed. *If you have any concerns or issues write them in a note and I will get a reply back to you in five to seven days.* There is not a dining room table to sit at any longer because it is only for décor in the house. They just sit in front of the TV set and eat.

No one communicates any longer. It's no wonder no one knows what their spouse is doing or even what the kids do when you aren't around. Maybe the lack of closeness in a family unit is where all this pent up anger and lack of self-worth comes from in the children. Maybe this is why most are so obsessed with death. Who knows what the future hold for us? The only concern I have is being eighty years old, looking at the new President of the United States on my TV saying "YO! I would just like to say Watz Up!!! And Fuck you very much to all my bitches and dogs that voted for me and have helped me get here today. I purpose I sell back half of the United States confiscated dope from the past two hundred years to the countries everybody bought them from for triple what they paid for it and then I'll just kick back and hang with my homies with the rest of the dope for the next four years".

The nightmare begins and I will be looking for the best last vacation spot to settle into for the worry-free life I have been looking for my whole life.

CHAPTER SIX

T.T.F.N.

This means "Ta Ta For Now" for those who are preppy illiterate, just like me. Life for me has been interesting to say the least, and the most I can say is that it's still running like a race car on the last lap at the track, looking for that checkered flag or the light at the end of the tunnel. There is never a dull moment it seems in my life, but it keeps everything lively and the laughter flowing. Just the other day my youngest daughter and I had to look for our first bra - not mine: hers. Not only did it have to look a certain way, but also it had to be silky. Thank God my daughter has lived with my sense of humor former twelve years of life, so what I had to say didn't shock or embarrass her. Since this bra had to be so special and we had actually found one we had to, of course, make sure it fit correctly.

While in the dressing room, I couldn't help but to notice the whole thing was made out of about a fourth of a yard of silky material, if that. The whole time I'm thinking this can't cost that much, so if she likes it, we will get it. Just as I was thinking this, I happened to see the price tag: $15.00!

I couldn't believe it. I turned to my daughter and said, *"Ya know, we could go to the first-aid department, get some Benadryl and Band Aides that should cure the swelling over-night and it won't cost any more than $3.00"*.

The lady in the next dressing room over was laughing hysterically, and my daughter just turned to me and said, *"Oh, Mom."*

See what happens when you grow up with humor? You don't even flinch. I'm sure I don't have to tell you what happened next. I bought the bra.

My children don't seem to be shocked by anything I say or do. It's almost as if it is as natural as sneezing, and someone blessing you directly after. It's nothing out of the ordinary for them.

I have refrained from yelling at my children or calling them names. I have always felt that talking with them and just trying to reason with them with a sense of humor was enough. I try to let them know they can talk to me about anything. and we can try to come up with a solution, if needed. I have also taught them how important it is sometimes to have your own personal space when you get frustrated. Some things don't need to be discussed. They just need quiet time to get over them.

I have learned a lot as well. Sometimes you don't expect them to remember what you teach them. I know, as an adult with a failing memory, I have forgotten much of what I had told them - things like the occasional need for personal space, for example - so I expected the children to forget, as well. Then my oldest daughter started walking off to her room during a discussion we were having and she said, *"Mom I just need a little space of my own right now."* In other words, she had about enough right now and my words of wisdom were frustrating her.

When she went to her room, I was thinking that she was disrespecting me and we needed to talk about her actions, so I started to walk down the hallway to her room to discuss this. But on the way to her room my middle daughter, sitting in the kitchen, said, *"I thought you said we should let you know when we needed our own space, Mom, no matter what was going on."*

I slowly turned to the washing machine and said, *"Yes, honey, that's why I am just getting the laundry out of the washer to put in the dryer."* There is nothing like an eight-year-old to remind you of what you had said at the last family meeting.

My children and the people who have surrounded me at work have always given me the laughter and the ammunition I needed to write this book. There was a time my daughter and her boyfriend were living with me and we only had one bathroom. Everyone was running late for work one day and getting ready at the same time, and I had to get my medicine from the bathroom, but my daughter's boyfriend was in the shower. I waited for as long as I could and finally just figured I would pop in for just a second and he would never know I was there. Just as I walked in, he turned off the shower and ripped back the curtain. The boy had a towel hanging above his head on the shower curtain rod but he obviously was in distress, because the first thing he picked up was a washcloth. He jumped around like a Mexican jumping bean, you know the ones in the clear little boxes with no place else to go, so they kind of bounce off the sides of the box? He was lifting one leg like a flamingo and trying to put that little washcloth somewhere. He tried every-thing in his power to figure out where to put it to cover the most area. My daughter and I started laughing and my daughter handed him the towel as I left the bathroom.

It's funny how people are raised to think that it is an embarrassing thing to be seen naked. I have taught my daughter that this is not a shameful thing. It's just how you were born. It's not something to freak out over. Everyone is different and sometimes you just can't be embarrassed about it. You have to learn to accept everyone for who they are. Appar-ently, my son-in-law-to-be was taught differently.

I think men have a harder time with this than women do. You would think all those years in the locker room in high school and streaking in front of the whole school at a football game would have cured them of this.

My youngest daughter was about ten or so when her father came out of the shower with a towel wrapped around him and walked out of the bathroom down the hall to his room. Something happened and he lost his towel along the way just as my daughter was coming around the corner with her snack from the kitchen on her way to her room. He picked up the towel and quickly wrapped himself up in it and just stood there quietly and frozen with fear. My daughter walked past him going to her room as if nothing major had happened and quickly remarked as she closed her door, *"I always wondered what you guys looked like."*

Since my second husband and I were divorced at this time, he ran to his room and called me on the phone, freaking out, *"She saw me naked. What should I do? Oh my God, how do I explain this? What happens now? What doe do?"*

I was laughing but felt sorry for him at the same time, so I asked him, *"What did shed? Did she freak out? Did she seem embarrassed?"*

He answered all the questions, *'no'*, and told me what she said. I let him know not to make a big deal out of this or it will affect how she thinks of herself. If she doesn't seem freaked out, don't give her any ammunition.

He and I are best friends still, despite the fact that when we were married, I had taken our marriage license off the wall just to see if they had replaced the word "obey" with "slave." We have always raised our daughter together but with my advice, so this was another learning curve for my ex-husband.

I have worked hard trying to write this book, sometimes thinking that I had my head spin like the girl on the movie, **"The Exorcists,"** just trying to make this book interesting enough for anyone to want to read no matter the gender. I feel I did well, considering I did not know what the hell I was doing. You know, it isn't like talking with your friends about all that has happened with your hands a going, with facial expressions and distinct sarcasm in your voice. In a book you can't do all that, so you really have to explain and give every last detail-pretty much what I call rambling on and on about everything I have ever found unusual or even funny.

At work the other day, we were discussing motherhood and the old wives' tales that go with it from other generations. A co-worker who was going to have a baby was contemplating breast-feeding, but didn't know what to do about how dry your nipples get. Another co-worker who had just had a baby said to put cabbage leaves on them and someone else said to put olive oil on them. I had said, *"And after all that you could make fried cabbage in the olive oil and serve it for dinner and tell your husband that dinner was made with a little bit of me in it."*

We laughed for a while on this one. Now, with all this wit and humor from everyone who knows who I am, comes the part where you, the readers come into play. If you should be blessed to read this book and like it, then I am more than ready to write another one, provided this one ever gets published.

If you're not a very humorous person, maybe this book will help you be a little humorous or it could rattle your chain to make others laugh from your ranting and raving.

I have lots more to write about parenting skills at their finest. There has to be at least two books on that topic. Look how many years you have invested with memories and thoughts about your children. Another book might be, *The Relationship Roulette Wheel: being on the rent-to-own plan before you get married.*

I'm sure there will be more books made out of whatever else strikes me as funny. Dealing with the public could be a book. And let's not forget all the e-mails you get from all kinds of people. For example, this was sent to me the other day: *WIFE VS HUSBAND--A married couple drive down a country road for several miles not saying a word. An earlier discussion had led to an argument, and neither of them wants to concede his or her position. As they passed a barnyard of mules, goats, and pigs, the husband asked sarcastically, "Relatives of yours?" "Yep," the wife replied, "in-laws."*

There should be a few funny things and experiences that go along with getting this book published which I'm sure that will end up in the next book. A lot of these companies want your life history and a resume; I'm just trying to figure out what they are going to get out of my resume. All mine says is how I have been a waitress most of my life, delivered auto parts, gone to school for teaching children, taught adults good parenting skills, dabbled in substance abuse counseling and data managing, and am now the proud owner of the title Case Manager for our women recovery home. So I'm not sure what they will find from my resume that qualifies me to be a first time writer.

I figure for the query letter I'll create something so catchy and humorous that they will all be asking to get a copy and read this book. When I figure out what it is I'm going to write to them, I will tell you in the next book so you don't miss anything good, okay? They just can't make it simple for you to give someone the book and let them say yes or no. There are all the policies and procedures that are written in Greek, so it takes you at least ten years to get your book to anyone at all. Surfing the web is not something I am good at so I keep picking people that want money I don't have to publish my book. If I had money, don't you think I would have already opened my own company and published my own book and the books of about fifty other people who can't figure any of this out either?

I have enjoyed writing this, though. It was like a little piece of me was put on paper, so if anything were to happen to me, everyone could at least re-member the sense of humor that made everyone around me laugh. I have even made myself laugh, writing all my memories down and re-living the events in my mind as I'm typing. Maybe if I get famous enough, you'll get to see me in person with all my sarcasm and facial expressions. You know I have tried that once. I probably told you somewhere in the book about how nervous I was, so I don't know how I would do with the whole world watch-ing. This book isn't very long, and I tend to worry about that being a problem getting it published, but at the same time it might be a perfect length for those of us with busy schedules and no time to read long, drawn out stories. Shoot, I barely had time to write this book. It has taken me six years, one boyfriend, and a husband just to get this much done. Yes, I have even left the one I had in the middle of this book, the one who couldn't keep his eyes off himself and his hands only on me. I just couldn't take the type of lifestyle he had and the moving in and out. Even in leaving this relationship, I did find sarcasm to help with the anger I had towards him.

He had stated to me that I needed to stop building these walls between us or our relationship was not going to survive. This is how unaware he was that his verbal, nasty, finger-pointing in my direction whenever he created a problem was what was causing the creation of the brick wall. After sitting there listening to him yell at me, all I could come up with was, *"Well, stop giving me the bricks to build it with because by the time you hand me the mortar, we are finished."* Apparently he didn't heed the sarcastic remark, because he handed me the mortar and it dried pretty quickly.

My friend from work tried to cheer me up and tell me that there are plenty of men out there dying to have someone treat them as I would, and would treat me in the same fashion. I was hoping deep inside that was true, but I had this mental picture in my head that I had met so many that I had wasted so much of my time that by the time I found the one that was dying to find me, he'd probably already have one foot in the grave, and the sight of me would give him a stroke on the first date.

Another friend of mine felt that I should stop fishing in the same dirty pond for the kind of men I keep catching. This was an interesting saying, but in order to stop fishing in the same pond I would have to move from Brevard County or chat on the Internet. I'm not so sure that the Internet is any better than the pond. What happens if you meet a jerk you just can't shake?

At work, my girlfriends and I ended up talking one day about *John Holmes* and this *Ron Jeremy* guy that is the hottest thing everyone says. He just doesn't give me that *"I want to rip my clothes off and take you"* attitude. It's more like, *put my clothes on and run out the door as fast as I can.*

Most people in life like to make love on a rug not to a rug.

On the other hand, some people like extremely furry people. There is a girl at work who is absolutely in love with Kermit the Frog and if he were a real person she would marry him and have tadpoles in a heartbeat.

Luckily, I didn't have to date long. In fact, I didn't date at all. My husband found me in a book at the library. I was home-schooling my oldest daughter, and I had her do research on Hitler and write an essay. When she returned the book, it had my new pager number in it so when my husband went to look up a date in it, he found the number. Out of curiosity he called it, and we have been together ever since. We even got married in the park next to the library.

I think, in writing this book, if they would have made a waterproof laptop computer then I could have taken some time in the tub to write, too; or used it through the three hurricanes we have been through. Yes, here in Florida the air is fresh with the scent of sawdust and the soothing sounds of saws

191

cutting plywood, with a hint of the hammering of nails to hold the plywood against the windows all around you. This, my friends, describes a very active hurricane season.

Driving around getting supplies, you see the wonderful sayings people have spray painted on their boarded up windows, *"Got Hurricane?"*... *"Here We Blow Again,"*... *"Insured by State Farm Smith and Wesson Protected."*

The wisdom and advice given to some during this stressful time is just as humorous. A co-worker talking to her mother was discussing how hard it was becoming to get plywood, and she didn't think her mother would have any luck in obtaining any. *"Just come to my house in Orlando* (50 Miles from Melbourne)" she told her mother, *"And don't worry about boarding up. You have insurance, right? Just let it blow out, Mom. What are you worried about?"*

This was funny. These storms put people in a lot of distress, and it is very hard finding humor when you are living without power for twelve days. But, yes, I did, at least for just a few minutes. With my luck, of course, within the first few hours of the first hurricane, we lost power. We had this little TV that you could plug into a cigarette lighter in a car, so while the storm was still pounding down on us, we wanted to see what was going on rather than listen to it on the radio. We went to the garage and plugged the little TV into the 1972 Monte Carlo. While standing on the outside of the car watching theta, I said it would be nice if we could sit down and watch it. We tried to put the TV on the dash but it was a little too fat to sit on the dash, so we put in on the hood close to the windshield, turned up the volume and sat inside the car. As we were watching the news, I started laughing and my husband thought that I had lost my mind. He said, *"What the hell are you laughing about? This isn't funny. They are saying that the eye of the storm is going to pass right over us."*

"I'm not laughing at that," I told him, *"I'm laughing because we are in a mini drive-in with no popcorn or fountain soda to put out on our windows."*

Needless to say, he still did not find humor in this but I thought it was great - our own little mini drive-in right in the garage.

These hurricanes were the best tests for how compatible you are. You and your other half really have to live in strained conditions for twelve days at a time. Who needs pre-marital counseling after this? I was under so much stress and finding out all of his nasty little habits and secrets that I couldn't stand looking at him any longer, and then to have to go through another hurricane one week later and survive another twelve days together was just too much. It was at the point where all you can do is thinking of how selfish, childish, and time-consuming he has been. Luckily, our marriage survived this entire nitpicking stage we went through.

I had to call FEMA for some assistance because my husband was out of work, and I had to pay all the bills. I was unable to do that because I'd used my paycheck to get provisions for the hurricane. While on the phone with the woman, explaining my situation to her, she had asked if I had any dependants.

I said, *"Since my husband is out of work and I pay all of the bills, can I claim him as a dependant?"*

She started laughing and said yes. After a few more digs at my husband and with some more questioning, the lady was now trying to stop laughing in order to read a clause that she had to be serious about while reading it to me. After three attempts, she said forget it and just read it to me while laughing. Someone from FEMA would be out to see me, and I would need to have proof of my living at this residence, and someone who was over the age of eighteen...., at this point she really lost it and couldn't continue. My comment that led to this hysterical laughter was, *"What if this someone is over the age of eighteen on a technicality, like his birth date, but mentally under fifteen? Will FEMA still think he qualifies?"*

"Then he shouldn't be the one there to answer the door," she laughed, *"So to help you out, they will call when they are on their way."*

I feel that I brightened that woman's day and probably the monotony that went along with angry people she had to deal with that day. I had to write letters to other companies because of their lack of compassion about the hurricane. Our phone bill was due the day the hurricane came in, and I didn't pay it because of what was happening, and dummy me thought they would have some understanding. The night we lost power, the phone line was ripped from the wall on the outside of the house. About four days into no-power-no phone, I receive a late-notice from the phone company stating they will be shutting our service off in three days, if not paid. I just started to laugh right there in front of the mailbox for all the neighbors to see.

You see, when I had called the phone company to report the phone line, they said it would be approximately three weeks before they would be able to have someone repair the line that was now on the ground. Threatening to turn the damn thing off when it was already turned off for five days and it didn't look like we were going to have phone service again until the end of the month was just... funny, asinine, and just plain uncompassionate. I wrote them a letter to try and get my point across to them without really pissing them off. God knows when we'd get our phone back then. *To Whom It May Concern: I have not had phone service since September 3rd and was told that it would be back on the 22nd. During this crisis I was sent a late notice for the phone bill. Because of not having funds to both have enough supplies for the hurricane and pay the bill by the 13th, I assumed this would not be a big problem for the caring people of BellSouth. This late notice to me was quite humorous since we had already been without a phone for the last 4 days and it appeared the phone would not be turned on until the end of the month. I mailed the bill payment on September 17th and would hope that I would not be charged a service fee. Due to other circumstances, I'd think we would not have a bill for the month of September, considering I wasn't able to use the phone or my Internet service for the month. I would like a reply of some sort from your company before you mail me out another monthly bill while the phone line is still lying in the back yard, wishing it could get out of the wet grass and back up in the box attached to the side of the house. Sincerely, Michelle Kismoky (Payer of this bill, even though it is in my husbands' name, due to his being out of work.)*

The outcome was they billed me for the whole month and a service charge to have the phone turned back on. I was on a roll so I decided to write the cable company as well.   *Hi! My name is Michelle and I am mailing you $100.00 of the $147.36. I will make it up to you on the next bill. I am also writing to you to let you know that our power has just been restored, and it looks like we still have cable but our line is hanging very low and has almost hung my husband while he was trying to mow the yard. Not that I am complaining that it almost hung him, but I was more concerned about his ripping it out and our therefore not having cable at all. The reason I am writing to you about this is we still have no phone and won't until September 22. Its line, too, was hanging in the backyard, but it actually has made it onto the ground. If this is some-*

thing you can fix and possibly credit our bill from September 3rd when the power went out, to September 14th when the power came on, that would be wonderful. Sincerely, Michelle Kismoky

The outcome was they credited us and never blinked an eye about a partial payment, nor did FPL. But Ma Bell, boy they are a tough cookie and if I had my way I probably would start my own phone company.

Time is a luxury most of us do not have as I have reminded each and every one of us in this book and, on the other side of the coin, if we have too much time it could be detrimental to our home life, as I have found out. I suspect with all the calls at work for anger management classes, everyone else has found out they had some compatibility issues of their own. There definitely has to be a balance.   Stopping and smelling the roses in this era means buy them at the convenient store with your cup of coffee and smell them while you're driving to work. I'm not sure which would be more overpowering, the French vanilla coffee or the roses. I think the coffee might win. So the next time you have time let's just say: stop and smell that cappuccino before it's all gone or before you spill it in your lap while driving, because some idiot just pulled out in front of you.

This did happen to me this morning and I was fixin' to get upset when God put some humor on the radio for me. The lady on the radio was talking about their having brains for sale now. You can get a female brain for fifty dollars or a male brain for two hundred dollars. I was thinking, *why is the male brains much more expensive*, and just as I asked, she began to say that the male replacement brain was more expensive because it was practically unused. This was cute enough to make me forget about going into work smelling like Shalimar with a touch of French vanilla cappuccino.

There are things that happen every day that I could write about. Just as I thought that I was finished with this book, I find myself adding more and more. The other day the office was taken to lunch at Carrabba's, a very nice Italian restaurant I had never been to before, but had always wanted to try. After placing my order, I went to the little girls' room. In most restaurants you have nice calming elevator music but in this bathroom they were playing an Italian lesson. You know, like the tapes you buy to learn Spanish where the bored guy's voice gives you the English word and the Spanish word for it.

I thought to myself that this was quite humorous that as I went pee I was able to learn Italian, without having to pay any more than what my lunch was going to cost. I thought it might only take six or seven trips to the bathroom in order to speak at least a short sentence, although I don't know what you would say to everyone at the table if you kept disappearing into the bathroom. Then I thought, if you could get your meal sent to the bathroom maybe you could learn more, but I sure that wouldn't look good either. Who knows, maybe if you visit that restaurant enough in a year, you might be able to have the basics to speak enough Italian to maybe even visit Italy to try it out.

Of course my husband feels that this is something only a redneck would think of – this from a man that can load a coffee maker with the water and the coffee but have to wait two hours for my friend's husband to come over to show him how to turn it on. Now, I ask you, which one of us sounds more like a redneck joke?

This difference brings me to another conversation at work about the way men adwomen think. A male co- worker had said why is it that women who have the ability to state their opinion are considered bitches but if a man has an opinion he is considered a free-thinker with well-thought-out ideas? And little do all his colleges know, it was the man's wife at home who gave him the thoughts before he left the house. I thought this was well thought out for a man to say this in front of a bunch of women at work, but after a little pondering I wonder if this thought came from his wife at home.

Just think: all this work for this book comes from years of people telling me, *"You're funny. You should write a book."*

For all those people:

HERE IT IS!!!!

This book is for you. No, I didn't say beer. I'll leave you with one more bit of humor. I was driving home from work today and a limo pulls up beside me at the stoplight. The rear window rolls down, and the young man inside with all his friends asks me, *"Pardon me would you happen to have some Grey Pupin in your glove box?"*

I started laughing and told him I was sorry but I'm all out. My friend was following me and we stopped at the corner store because I could not stop laughing. My friend was from Kentucky and couldn't hear what was said but she must have thought I was being harassed because this is what she asked when she came up to my car, *"Did they ask you if you and any panties on?"*

This made me laugh even harder and I think I even peed my panties. I think after all this I need a really good vacation. I was thinking that it would be really cool if you could go to some place like Disney, only better. You could spend a week as someone else with someone else's problems, so you could have a vacation get away from yourself. I would like to be *June Cleaver* for a week. The only problem is I think my husband wants to be *Clint Eastwood.*

Maybe when I get rich and famous I can create a theme park just for that purpose, like a time machine. You could pick the time period you would like to visit. At the gate you would pay your fee, give up your cell phone, palm pilots, computers and begin the vacation with the clothes and transportation needed for the year. The home you would stay in would also be set up for the time. Prices for things would be of that time and the labeling for the merchandise would also be authentic to the year. This would be a wonderful vacation spot, I would think.

While I'm at it, I think I will open a clothing store for the fuller-figure women where you could feel smaller without being smaller. Let's say if you are a size sixteen, like I am, you would just add the one and six together and you are instantly a size seven. A woman that is a size twenty-two would be a size four. I think women would feel better about buying clothes in their size if it looked as if they were getting a smaller size.

These are some ideas I kick around that hopefully will come true just like my dream for this book to be published.

Well, until we encounter each other again, enjoy your life, and try to find a little humor in your day. By the way I have had to throw another trashcan away. So let me leave you with his final words.

Hi! I am yet another one of this woman's trash cans that needs to retire so I will need a ride. I have served her well the last few years, come rain or shine or the occasional new guy that emptied me into the truck and didn't throw me far enough into the yard to prevent me from rolling out on the street and getting run over. Regardless of all that, I did my job, always coming out full of goodies with every intention of coming back empty and uncrushed to be filled up again to go back out the next week. But, alas, all the amateur NASCAR drives driving down the street have ran over me one too many times and I am unable to keep my shape or stand up straight,(plastic osteoporosis, it happens in our old age) or hold my goodies too well any longer. So here I am for you to take me to my final resting place and away from NASCAR tryouts on this street. Thank you for the ride, and you all have a wonderful day. Sincerely, Another Retired Trash Can.

Meet Our Author

MICHELLE KISMOKY

In Her Own Words

I was born on May 18th 1966 at Wright Patterson Air Force Base in Fairborn, Ohio. Yes, this is also were they keep the aliens in secret warehouses on base. I often feel that I could have been switched at birth with how I think sometimes. I have three wonderful daughters and one fantastic granddaughter and a handsome grandson. No, I am not a grandmother, that sounds too old for a young woman of 30, for the first time this year after being 29 for ten years in a row, I am Nana. I have always had a great sense of humor no matter how bad things were in my life.

I have had life-altering changes thoughout my life, sexual and physical abuse as a child, divorce, my house broken into and beaten to almost an inch of my life, divorce again and lastly breast cancer. These are not life experiences that are easy to move on from but my strong will and humor has kept me going. I did go to college thru all of this and received a vocational degree in early childhood development and went on to teach little ones for a few years.

After desperately seeking adult conversation and needing to be a grown-up again I went to work for an organization that teaches adults how to parent so I sort of stayed in my field that I went to school for. I have absorbed and learn all aspects of the company I work for and now I am their Case Manager for the Recovery home. I enjoy my job but my best love of all is making the people I work with laugh at least once a day.

Life may not be a bed of roses but I love red roses so I keep them around me at all times so I am sure to smell the flowers everyday no matter what that day may hold for me.

Writing this book I feel was the best way to express my vision of life with everyone and get him or her to laugh too.

Enjoy Life.